CHINA IN A GLOBALIZING WORLD

UNITED NATIONS
New York and Geneva
2005

NOTE

The views expressed in this book are those of the authors and do not necessarily reflect the views of the UNCTAD secretariat. The designations employed and the presentation of the material do not imply the expression of any opinion whatsoever on the part of the Secretariat of the United Nations concerning the legal status of any country, territory, city or area, or of its authorities, or concerning the delimitation of its frontiers or boundaries.

*
* *

Material in this publication may be freely quoted; acknowledgement, however, is requested (including reference to the document number). It would be appreciated if a copy of the publication containing the quotation were sent to the Publications Assistant, Division on Globalization and Development Strategies, UNCTAD, Palais des Nations, CH-1211 Geneva 10.

UNCTAD/GDS/MDPB/2005/1

UNITED NATIONS PUBLICATIONS
Sales No.E.05.II.D.23
ISBN 92-1-112683-5

FOREWORD

China's impressive economic achievements over the past two decades have made its development experiences quite distinct from those of many other economies. Its robust economic growth has dramatically reduced poverty, making it the most important driving force towards achieving the United Nations Millennium Development Goal of halving world poverty by 2015.

The speed of China's progression from a low-income and populous country to a global economic force has taken many analysts by surprise. Academics and policy-makers in the developed and developing world have therefore been examining the "China phenomenon" and its impact on regional and world economies. They have analysed key issues such as the factors and determinants of China's catching-up strategy, how the Chinese model differs from previous development models, and the extent to which other developing countries might emulate the Chinese economic model and the impact of China's economic growth on regional and world economies.

In China itself, policy-makers are asking themselves how the country's rapid economic growth can be sustained; how welfare benefits for the Chinese population can be enhanced; how to close the considerable remaining gap between China and the world's leading economies within the shortest possible time; and how to redress socioeconomic inequality within the country. China is fully aware that it faces a number of development challenges: external pressure on currency revaluation is mounting; financial reform is far from complete; existing bottlenecks risk slowing down rapid growth; income inequality is proving difficult to redress; and a social safety net has yet to be established.

It was against this backdrop of domestic and international policy development research that the Ministry of Commerce of China (MOFCOM) came to an agreement with UNCTAD to explore some of the key issues relating to China's development path in an increasingly globalizing world. UNCTAD has closely followed and analysed developments in China, while also extending technical assistance. Promoting sustainable and equitable economic development and supporting the beneficial integration of developing countries into the global economy are at the core of UNCTAD's mission. This study of the economic issues of immediate concern to China and the rest of the world provides a welcome opportunity to enhance UNCTAD's existing partnership with the Chinese Government, as well as with Chinese policy makers and academics.

This book comprises a selection of presentations made at seminars jointly organized by UNCTAD and MOFCOM, with the participation of the Asian Development Bank Institute. Work on the project is ongoing and UNCTAD looks forward to further fruitful outcomes of this close collaboration.

Carlos Fortin
Officer-in-Charge of UNCTAD

ACKNOWLEDGEMENTS

This publication is a collection of presentations made at various seminars organized by UNCTAD and the Ministry of Commerce of China within the context of their joint Project on Managing Globalization and Economic Integration.

The papers included herein do not necessarily reflect the views of the United Nations, or the Ministry of Commerce of China.

The cover was designed by Diego Oyarzun.

ABOUT THE AUTHORS

Jiyao Bi, Deputy Director, Institute for International Economic Research, National Development and Reform Commission of the People's Republic of China.

Sebastian Dullien, Financial Times Deutschland. Paper prepared during a short-term employment with UNCTAD.

Heiner Flassbeck, Officer-in-Charge, UNCTAD Division on Globalization and Development Strategies.

Michael Geiger, Assistant Economic Affairs Officer, UNCTAD Division on Globalization and Development Strategies.

Yuefen Li, Senior Economic Affairs Officer, UNCTAD Division on Globalization and Development Strategies. Manager of the Project on Managing Globalization and Economic Integration.

Hong Song, Associate Professor, Institute of World Economics and Politics, Chinese Academy of Social Sciences.

Yuanjian Sun, Director, Department of International Trade and Economic Affairs, Ministry of Commerce of the People's Republic of China.

John Weiss, Director of Research, Asian Development Bank Institute.

Chai Yu, Senior Researcher, Institute of Asia Pacific Studies, Chinese Academy of Social Sciences.

CONTENTS

CHINA'S SPECTACULAR GROWTH SINCE THE MID-1990S – MACROECONOMIC CONDITIONS AND ECONOMIC POLICY CHANGES

Heiner Flassbeck, in collaboration with Sebastian Dullien and Michael Geiger

GLOBALIZATION AND THE INTEGRATION OF CHINA INTO THE WORLD ECONOMY
Yuanjiang Sun

CHINA AND ITS NEIGHBOURS: PARTNERS OR COMPETITORS FOR TRADE AND INVESTMENT?
John Weiss

WHY IS CHINA THE WORLD'S NUMBER ONE ANTI-DUMPING TARGET?
Yuefen Li

Figure

Table

CHINA'S NEW CONCEPT FOR DEVELOPMENT
Jiyao Bi

Figure

FDI IN CHINA: TRENDS AND MACROECONOMIC CHALLENGES
Sebastian Dullien

MARKET OPENING, ENTERPRISE LEARNING AND INDUSTRY TRANSFORMATION – A CASE STUDY OF CHINA'S CAR INDUSTRY
Hong Song, Chai Yu

Table

ACRONYMS AND ABBREVIATIONS

AD	anti-dumping
ADB	Asian Development Bank
ADBI	Asian Development Bank Institute
ASEAN	Association of Southeast Asian Nations
CEO	Chief Executive Officer
CES	creative electronic systems
CGE	computable general equilibrium model
CSRC	China Securities and Regulatory Commission
EEF	Engineering Employer's Federation of the United Kingdom
FDI	foreign direct investment
GATT	General Agreement on Tariffs and Trade
GDP	gross domestic product
HS	Harmonized System
IMF	International Monetary Fund
MDGs	Millennium Development Goals
MFN	Most Favoured Nation
MNE	multinational enterprises
MOFCOM	Ministry of Commerce of China
MOL	Ministry of Labour of China
NIE	newly industrializing economy
NME	non-market economy
OECD	Organisation for Economic Co-operation and Development
PBC	People's Bank of China
R&D	research and development
RCA	revealed comparative advantage
RDVA	relative depth-of-value-added
REER	real effective exchange rate
RMB	Renminbi
SARS	Severe Acute Respiratory Syndrome
SITC	Standard International Trade Classification
SOE	state-owned enterprise
TNCs	transnational corporations
ULC	unit labour cost
UNCTAD	United Nations Conference on Trade and Development
VAT	value added tax
WDI	World Development Indicators
WTO	World Trade Organization

CHINA'S SPECTACULAR GROWTH SINCE THE MID-1990S – MACROECONOMIC CONDITIONS AND ECONOMIC POLICY CHALLENGES

Heiner Flassbeck
in collaboration with Sebastian Dullien and Michael Geiger[1]

Abstract

This paper analyses the macroeconomic reasons for the Chinese boom since the mid-1990s. It is argued that the stable growth performance of China would not have been possible without the strategy of unilaterally fixing the exchange rate, which has been implemented since 1994. This strategy was successful because it was accompanied by a reform of the wage-setting regime in the mid-1990s, a heterodox macroeconomic demand management that has addressed the country's needs and a rather closed capital account. This arrangement has made it possible for China to both master the challenges of globalization and modernize the domestic economy at the same time. Without this macroeconomic complement to favourable microeconomic conditions, it is argued, the stable and vigorous growth of the past decade would not have been possible.

INTRODUCTION

The economic performance of China over the past 30 years has been impressive. Since the beginning of the reform phase in 1979, per capita income has risen fivefold; average private consumption today is roughly 400 per cent above the level at the beginning of the reforms in real terms. China was able to lift more than 200 million people out of absolute poverty (World Bank 1997). Its total GDP in dollar terms is already close to that of Italy, Britain or France, and its GDP in purchasing power parities might already be higher than that of Germany. With growing speed China has opened its market and made a quick integration into the world economy possible. While the country was virtually closed to international trade at the end of the 1970s, it has now managed to overtake France and Japan, the world's

---

[1] The opinions expressed in this paper are those of the authors and do not necessarily reflect the views of UNCTAD. The authors remain solely responsible for any shortcomings in this paper.

fourth and third biggest exporter in 2003, respectively (WTO 2004). China has likewise become an important global player in an increasing number of industries. As a result, China is now a major power in international economic policy. This is reflected in the fact that international finance and exchange-rate movements cannot sensibly be discussed without including China in the discussions.

The whole growth and catching-up period can be split into two different sub-periods. China grew rapidly but unspectacularly compared with other successful Asian economies from the end of the 1970s to the beginning of the 1990s, however the pace of catching-up has accelerated markedly since 1994 (Table 1). Recently, the Chinese economy has seemed to shoot through the roof with growth rates ranging between 8 and 9.5 per cent since 2002. The overall investment ratio is close to 50 per cent with an apparently never-ending exceptional construction boom; FDI is still flowing in on a large scale and the growth of exports and imports is breathtaking.

Economic literature explains the extraordinary growth performance of the Chinese economy mainly by specific microeconomic reforms in the transition process. Traditionally, observers examine how the overall reform process was brought forward and specify qualitatively the efficiency gains brought forward by single reform measures. In the late 1990s, a wide range of articles and books explored China's growth experience: Some of them stressed the gradualist reform approach and the appearance of new, non-capitalist institutions as the main characteristic of the Chinese model. Others compared the Chinese experience with other successful catching-up periods in Asia, focusing on the gradual convergence of existing institutions towards those prominent in the Asian model (for an overview see Sachs and Woo 1997). Overall, these explanations of the "Chinese miracle" are not conclusive. From the very beginning, China was less of a "market-fundamentalist" than other transition countries and much less consequent in transforming its institutions into what the Washington consensus considers as the only promising systemic departure from the old state-dominated model. Moreover, even if the undeniable success of the Asian model suggests that it has created successful institutions and regulations, it is by no means evident that regional affiliation is sufficient to explain any national success by the institutions that have been associated with the Asian model.

This paper explores a different path. While it acknowledges the role of market- based reforms in putting in place the necessary conditions for strong economic growth, it will principally focus on and analyse the macroeconomic conditions that made it possible for China to grow vigorously over such a long period of time. The paper argues that China's undeniable success in igniting and sustaining growth from 1994 onwards was the result of a policy package that combined market-orientated, but prudent microeconomic reforms, with aggressive and growth-oriented macroeconomic policies. In the 1990s, no country in the world achieved to combine a stable and competitive exchange rate, a low interest rate level and an anti-cyclical fiscal demand management with a low inflation environment. China, however, in the aftermath of the inflation and exchange-rate shock in 1994, managed to combine an aggressive pro-growth monetary policy with a high degree of price stability. Chinese authorities kept the inflation rate under control through the use of heterodox instruments such as wage and price controls. The policy was complemented by capital controls, non-orthodox investment policies and an active fiscal policy.

Foreign Direct Investment (FDI) has played an important supporting role as it helped China to integrate into a regional production network, thereby speeding up the country's technological integration into the world economy. However, given the favourable overall investment environment created by the policy package, FDI inflows have not been central to China's success.

In a nutshell, China's performance since 1994 has been the result of the working of the profit-investment nexus,[2] the interplay of pro-growth monetary conditions with vigorous export growth and a very stable domestic demand-development. Extremely favourable monetary conditions boosted capital accumulation. Investment, fuelled by quickly rising non-equilibrium profits,[3] has been the main driver of growth; a good export-performance and high growth rates of real income and demand of households have been the main stabilizers of overall growth.

---

[2] Keynes (1930); UNCTAD *Trade and Development Report* (various issues).
[3] Flassbeck (2004).

This paper is organized as follows: Section I outlines some stylized facts on China's economic development in an Asian and Latin American perspective. Section II gives some indication on the interaction of traditional policy instruments with non-orthodox monetary instruments. Section III describes the role of FDI in the development process and Section IV presents a number of policy conclusions.

I. CHINA'S GROWTH PERFORMANCE IN PERSPECTIVE

Though impressive by itself and particularly in relation to Latin American or African countries, China's long-run economic performance is not extraordinary compared to other Asian countries that have experienced rapid catch-up growth in the course of the 20th century.[4] Table 1 lists major growth episodes of Asian countries experiencing annual GDP per capita growth above 7 per cent over recent decades. Obviously, neither the Chinese GDP per capita growth nor the rate of investment is markedly higher than other countries: Both Japan and Korea experienced long periods of more than ten consecutive years of GDP per capita growth in excess of 5 per cent. In all these countries and episodes, the average investment share was above 25 per cent of GDP; China's share of almost 37 per cent between 1994 and 2003 was, however, outstanding.

In these episodes the three countries achieved per capita growth rates between 7.2 and 9.1 per cent (Figure 1). However, all but China (1994–2003) are characterized by high volatile growth rates in their growth episodes. China's (1994–2003) highest/lowest growth rates were 11.33/6.18, while Japan (1961–1973) and the Republic of Korea (1968–1979) show a much wider deviation of 12.51/4.69 and 11.64/2.77, respectively.

I.1.   Exports and the external balance

The speed with which China penetrated world markets is not unprecedented either. During the first years of China's reform period initiated by Deng Xiaoping, export growth in China was significantly

---

[4] For a similar evaluation, see IMF (2004).

slower than in other Asian countries during their catch-up periods (Rumbaugh/Blancher 2004). Figure 2 illustrates this point. While the Republic of Korea doubled its exports within four years following the take-off of exports in 1968, China needed the ten-year period until 1990 to increase its exports by "just" around 50 per cent compared to 1981. But since the mid-1990s the Chinese export growth has accelerated; after 1994 it took China only seven years to double its exports, even though the initial level in 1994 was 2.6 times higher than in 1981. Since 2000, Chinese exports have, by far, outpaced the performance of other countries in comparable periods. China almost doubled its exports in the three years from 2000 to 2003.

The development of imports reflects similar patterns during all the periods of high growth experienced by the countries under consideration (Figure 3).

Despite recent rapidly growing imports to China, large external surpluses seem to be a rather common feature of Asia's growth experiences. The Republic of Korea's surplus from 1983 to 1991 averaged at 1.3 per cent of GDP; Japan's surplus from 1961 to 1973 reached 0.7 per cent of GDP; and Hong Kong (China) achieved a staggering surplus of 7 per cent in the early 1970s. China recorded an average current account surplus of 2 per cent between 1994 and 2002 (WDI Online 2005).

The only major period of strong Asian growth with persistent current account deficits is the early growth period of the Republic of Korea which occurred between 1968 and 1973. The Republic of Korea's current account deficit at the time averaged 7.2 per cent of GDP. However, this large deficit was mainly a structural deficit, which the Republic of Korea had inherited from the 1950s; particularly, grain imports with small price elasticity contributed to the import surplus. At the time policy-makers in the Republic of Korea actively fought the deficit by stimulating exports and discouraging imports (Hong 1998). However, the country's high dependence on capital goods imports during the export promotion phase meant that the deficit was quite persistent. By contrast, the Chinese deficit of the 1980s was moderate in size and rather volatile compared to the structural nature of the Republic of Korea's deficit. In China, a deficit of about 4 per cent in 1985 was replaced by a surplus of about 3 per cent in 1990.

Table 1
MAIN ASIAN GROWTH EPISODES

Country	Period	Length (years)	Average annual GDP per capita growth (in per cent)	Average annual exports (as a percentage of GDP)	Average annual investment[1] (as a percentage GDP)	Average annual consumption (as a percentage GDP)
China	1981–1988	8	9.1	10.5	29.3	65.4
China	1994–2003	10	7.9	25.1	36.7	58.0
Japan	1961–1973	13	8.5	10.0	33.1	63.4
Republic of Korea	1968–1979	12	7.2	22.2	26.8	79.5
Republic of Korea	1983–1991	9	8.0	32.6	31.5	66.8

Source: World Bank, *World Development Indicators* (WDI).
[1] Measured as growth rate of gross fixed capital formation (GFCF).

Figure 1
GDP PER CAPITA GROWTH, INITIAL + 10 YEARS

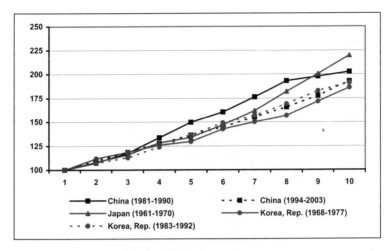

Source: World Bank, *World Development Indicators.*

Figure 2
EXPORT PERFORMANCES IN CHINA, JAPAN AND THE REPUBLIC OF KOREA

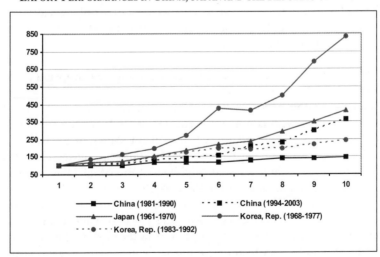

Source: World Bank, *World Development Indicators.*

Figure 3
DEVELOPMENTS OF IMPORTS IN CHINA, JAPAN AND THE REPUBLIC OF KOREA

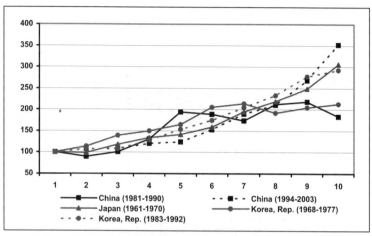

Source: World Bank, *World Development Indicators.*

From an Asian perspective, the pattern of Chinese foreign trade in the 1980s was an exception, while the trade pattern in the 1990s mirrors that of the traditional Asian growth experience. It is only recently that China began to record bouts in exports and imports that went far beyond the historical experience.

I.2. Domestic developments: investment and consumption

Similarly to the export pattern, China's performance in terms of domestic investment is not unprecedented in an Asian context either. Whereas, in a global perspective investment shares of 29.3 (in the 1980s) and 36.7 per cent (from 1994 to 2003) are outstanding, the performances of China's Asian neighbours were comparable. Japan's average investment share from 1961 to 1973 amounted to 33.1 per cent of its GDP. The Republic of Korea's investment ratio reached 31.5 per cent of GDP between 1983 and 1991. A comparison of the ten-year episode shows a similar pattern in the first 7 years of each period (Figure 4). As mentioned above, China's performance in the 1990s was less volatile than in the 1980s when investment growth fell after 8 years.

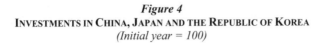

Figure 4
INVESTMENTS IN CHINA, JAPAN AND THE REPUBLIC OF KOREA
(Initial year = 100)

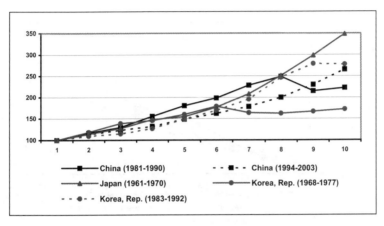

Source: World Bank, *World Development Indicators.*

China's performance with regard to private consumption resembles the traditional Asian pattern for the whole catching-up period since the beginning of the period of reforms (Figure 5). While consumption grew at a slower pace than GDP at the beginning of the growth acceleration in all the observed episodes, the size and the stability of the growth rates of private consumption are still remarkable: In all the countries and periods of catching-up, the real growth rate of the expenditure of private households consistently exceeded 8 per cent. Between 1994 and 2003, real private consumption expenditure in China rose by more than 9 per cent per year. This mirrors the developments in the Republic of Korea and Japan as well as in China during the first reform era (WDI Online 2005).

For China, as for the rest of Asia, the strong growth in consumption was associated with an adequate growth of real wages. For example, from 1994 to 2002 nominal wages in Chinese manufacturing, including bonuses and additional payments, rose by an annual rate of 12.5 per cent. Even after allowing for an annual inflation rate of 3.1 per cent (measured with the consumer price index), this leaves an annual real wage increase of more than 8 per cent. Similar wage increases are recorded in the services and finance sectors. Even though employment in these sectors covers a relatively small part of

Figure 5
CONSUMPTION GROWTH IN CHINA, JAPAN AND THE REPUBLIC OF KOREA
(Initial year = 100)

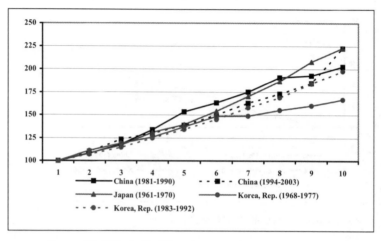

Source: World Bank, *World Development Indicators.*

Figure 6
WAGE INCREASE AND PRODUCTIVITY GROWTH IN CHINESE MANUFACTURING

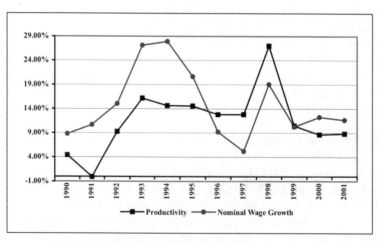

Source: Authors' calculations based on World Bank, *World Development Indicators* and ILO, *LABORSTA.*

the working population (according to official statistics, almost half of the labour force still works in agriculture), the stable real wage rates enabled a significant increase of purchasing power of private households. Recently, people living in rural areas have also experienced an increase of their purchasing power, spurred by wage increases in urban areas. This is explained by the fact that firms in certain areas and sectors, e.g. the construction sector, rely heavily on rural migrant workers who commute back and forth to their home areas and thereby increase the purchasing power there. The remittances of urban populations to relatives in rural areas play an increasingly important role. Certainly, while the flow of funds into the poorer regions is not sufficient to prevent the income gap between urban and rural population from widening, it does help to explain the growth in consumption throughout the whole country over the past decade.

All in all, strong consumption and investment growth explain the virtuous circle China entered at an early stage of its development experience: High investment triggered rapid productivity growth and allowed for suitable wage and profit increases (Figure 6) without jeopardizing international competitiveness and domestic price stability. Consumption and export growth in turn created new incentives to invest. Some simple econometric evidence shows that investment is rather strongly correlated to the growth of private domestic expenditure (see Table 2 and below). Thus, it appears that the interaction between buoyant domestic and external demand in an environment of extremely stable and accommodative interest-rate and exchange-rate conditions is crucial to understanding China's investment dynamics and its capital accumulation in the 1990s.

I.3.   Price and exchange-rate developments

Price and exchange-rate developments in China have to be split into two distinct episodes over recent decades. The first period, ranging from 1987 to 1994, was characterized by highly volatile monetary conditions with inflation reaching peaks of almost 20 per cent in 1988 and close to 25 per cent in 1994. The exchange rate was devalued in several steps. After 1994, however, the inflation rate fell dramatically and has been stabilized around the zero line, sometimes even indicating deflationary pressure. The nominal exchange rate before

Figure 7
INFLATION AND NOMINAL EXCHANGE RATE, 1987–2002

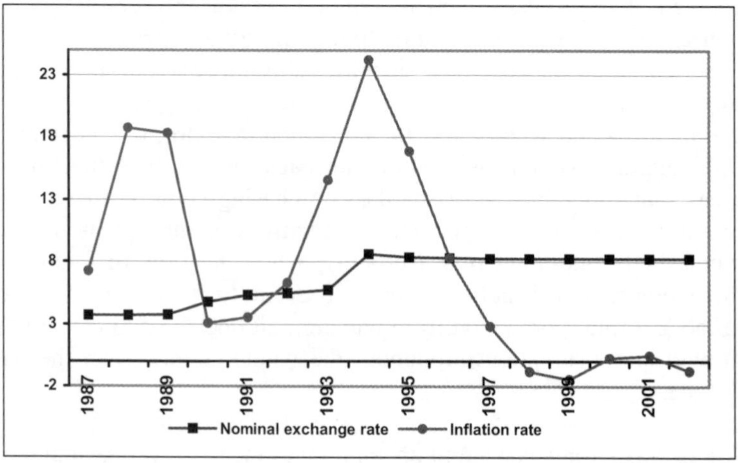

Source: IMF, *International Financial Statistics.*

1994 has been frequently adjusted within a system of multiple exchange rates and strong exchange-rate controls. After 1994 the Renminbi (RMB) remained stable to the United States Dollar. From 1994 to mid-1995 the exchange rate appreciated from RMB8.7/US$1 to RMB8.3/US$1. Since then the exchange rate was kept stable at a rate of RMB8.3/US$1. Eventually, in the wake of the Asian crisis a de facto peg at RMB8.28/US$1 was established (Figure 7).

Placed with a longer-term perspective, the decision of the Chinese authorities to peg the nominal exchange rate against the dollar after a strong devaluation in 1994 represented an attempt, once and for all, to abandon the volatile monetary conditions and the danger of monetary destabilization that had shaped the 1980s. The real exchange rate based on unit labour costs,[5] the broadest measure of international competitiveness, fell drastically after 1994 when the dual exchange-rate system was abandoned (Figure 8) and has since remained at a rather low rate. The devaluation in 1994 and the absolute fixing

---

[5] For an explanation of the concept of the real exchange rate based on unit labour cost, see UNCTAD (2004).

Figure 8
DIFFERENT MEASURES FOR CHINA'S REAL EFFECTIVE EXCHANGE RATE

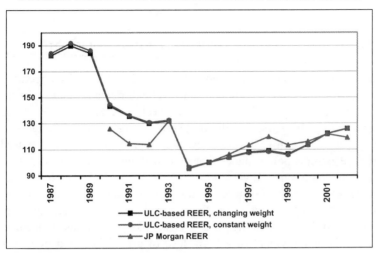

Sources: JP Morgan; authors' calculations.

of the Chinese RMB to the US$ in 1998 constitute a key factor in China's macroeconomic management and its extraordinary growth performance.

A somewhat similar approach can be found in other success stories in Asia. The Republic of Korea devalued its currency in the early 1960s by almost 50 per cent and defended its favourable position afterwards with a crawling peg arrangement, allowing a domestic rate of inflation above the United States rate without losing competitiveness. According to several studies, Japan (in the same way as Germany and some other European countries) entered the Bretton Woods system with a very favourable currency valuation (Williamson 1999), and kept domestic inflation reasonably low to defend this position in subsequent years.

By contrast, China's exchange rate management in the 1980s can hardly be considered a success story as the country neither had a competitive real exchange rate nor did it try to increase its competitiveness by managing the exchange rate. Instead, the official exchange rate was most likely significantly overvalued as was indicated by the large spread between the official and the swap market rate over much of that period.

II. CHINA'S SUCCESSFUL HETERODOX POLICY MIX

Since 1994, China's special policy mix of a stable and competitive exchange rate and a prudent anti-cyclical demand management, flanked by very stable and low, real interest rate level, is outstanding.[6] In particular, the unilateral fixing of the exchange rate at a very competitive level reflected a degree of investment-biased macroeconomic policy stance that remained unrivaled in the 1990s, in fact there are only a very few examples in earlier periods. The objective raised against an excessive use of monetary stimulation is the inflationary danger normally invoked by such an arrangement under traditional, Washington consensus-like, conditions. Indeed, in China the employment of a high dose of growth-oriented monetary policies was made possible by a successful implementation of non-orthodox instruments, including several types of incomes' policy and wage controls (see Section II.2 for a detailed discussion of the wage regime). The Chinese authorities were able to manage the inflation rate with non-orthodox instruments to free monetary policy from the strict obligation of inflation control without sacrificing the inflation target as such.

The development of nominal and real lending rates in China from 1994 to 2003 is telling (Figure 9). Due to high inflation rates in 1994 and 1995, the short-term real interest rate was negative until the new monetary regime took over. After the devaluation in 1994, nominal interest rates came down and real rates went up. Both remained at a very stable positive level throughout the 1990s. With real lending rates of between 4 and 7 per cent between 1997 and 2003 in an economy that was growing briskly at rates of 8 to 10 per cent, monetary policy was clearly accommodative. The second remarkable aspect of this way of managing monetary policy in an opening economy was the stability of interest rates. Even during the turmoil of

---

[6] UNCTAD (2004).

the Asian crisis in 1997 and 1998 stable real and nominal rates ensured that the pro-growth approach remained on track.

Figure 9
NOMINAL AND REAL INTEREST RATES, 1994–2003

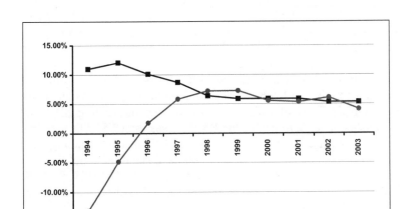

Source: Authors' calculations based on IMF, *International Financial Statistics*.

II.1. The exchange-rate regime and its influence on exports and capital accumulation

The main element of China's successful strategy came in 1994 when it shifted to a radically new exchange-rate regime. Until 1994, two exchange rates existed: An official rate and a rate in the swap market, where firms could trade their foreign exchange against domestic currency.[7] Under this scheme domestic enterprises had to hand over a share of their foreign earnings at the official exchange rate, but were allowed to trade the rest in the swap market. By means of a number of strong nominal depreciations, the official rate was brought down

---

[7] In fact, the development of the swap market took several years, and only from the early 1990s onwards a unified and liquid swap market existed (cf. Lin/Schramm, 2003).

close to the swap rate before the two were unified in 1994 at a rather low level and the dual system was replaced by an arrangement resembling a crawling peg – the exchange rate was allowed to fluctuate within a narrow daily band – which still is in place today. With relatively larger trading bands between 1994 and 1996 the crawling peg arrangement was used and the RMB appreciated slightly from RMB8.7 per US$ in 1994 to RMB8.3 per US$ in 1996. Since 1997 and the Asian financial crises, China has maintained a *de facto* peg of the RMB to the US$ with very small variations. According to Anderson (2003) the peg needs to have the add-on of *de facto* or *quasi*, since the official regulation still allows the RMB to fluctuate within a certain bandwidth.[8] Facing the outbreak of the Asian crises, the People's Bank of China (PBC) narrowed the trading band and established a *de facto* peg of the RMB versus the US$ with a trading band of 0.4 per cent around the RMB8.28/US$ peg. The trading band was further tightened in November 2000 and stands at about 0.01 per cent fluctuation around the central parity of RMB8.277/US$. Still, the RMB is not completely fixed, but the actual trading band is very narrow at the moment.

Overall competitiveness of the Chinese economy, measured by the real exchange rate against the main trading partners, improved by almost 50 per cent between 1987 and 1994. Unit labour costs in dollar terms fell in China during this time and the currencies of main trading partners, such as Japan or Germany, appreciated strongly against the dollar. Although the actual impact of the change in competitiveness differs according to the underlying measurement (e.g. the IMF and JP Morgan base their indices on consumer or industrial prices instead of unit labour costs), the general conclusion of all studies remains the same. Due to productivity increases, adequate wage growth and the strong nominal devaluation in 1994, China has been able to increase its competitiveness significantly. The steep increase in exports discussed in Section I underlines the fact that the nominal depreciation of the exchange rate in combination with the non-inflationary reaction of other cost variables, mainly nominal wages and other stabilizing heterodox macroeconomic policy instruments, constituted a breakthrough for Chinese exporters and foreign firms producing or planning to produce in China.

---

[8] Anderson (2003), p. 4.

Nevertheless, for a lasting achievement in terms of growth and catching-up it is critical to turn the export success into a process of sustained capital accumulation. In China, the expectation of steady and pro-growth macroeconomic conditions, combined with an expanding domestic market in a non-inflationary environment, offered domestic and international investors the kind of stable profit expectations needed for investment in fixed capital on a large scale.[9] International investors were attracted to bring in capital-intensive production processes from their home countries and combine it with the cheap Chinese labour. Servén (2002) provides empirical evidence for the stability bias of international investors. For example, in his sample of developing countries, private investment reacts negatively to an increase in real exchange-rate volatility. Moreover, the author shows that private investment is particularly negatively affected in countries that experience large, real exchange-rate gyrations as a result of high inflation rates or distinctive nominal exchange-rate volatility.

China has managed to achieve a real exchange rate position, sometimes referred to as "optimal path of real exchange rate" movements, for a developing country that aims at industrialization (Larraín 1999). Accordingly, after an initial devaluation, the real exchange rate should only be allowed to recover gradually; and that is exactly what happened in China since the early 1990s. After an initial large devaluation, the real, effective exchange rate has until recently remained on a relatively stable but flat upward trend.

However, the stable and competitive position of the Chinese economy not only serves as an investment incentive for exporters but also helped domestic private companies obtain (extra) finance for their (new) investment projects. As domestic private companies in China still face higher barriers in accessing bank credits than state-owned enterprises (SOEs), they have traditionally relied heavily on internal

---

[9] This argument is in line with a recent contribution to the theory of investment (Dixit and Pindyck 1994). They show that increasing volatility can lead to less investment if a significant part of the investment is irreversible and deviations from a constant return-of-scale/competitive market model are allowed. This is obviously increasingly the case where the more training the production of a certain good requires. Thus, investments in skill-intensive and capital-intensive (as the workers have to learn to use the capital) production lines are most likely to be affected by higher volatility.

finance – a situation that still exists to this day.[10] Thus, increased competitiveness after 1994 has helped them earn extra profits through increased export shares and/or higher profit margins, which in turn build the basis for the internal financing of new investments.

The effects of the pro-growth monetary policy stance in China can be shown empirically. Estimating an aggregate investment function shows that the overall investment can be reasonably well explained by private consumption-induced demand, the demand for Chinese exports, the real interest rate and a dummy for the period from 1995 onward. The empirical investment function of Table 2 shows that the 1994/1995 shift of macroeconomic policy towards a more expansionary stance had a highly significant positive effect on investment. The table reveals that the overall outcome of the policy shift could be compared to the effect of a permanent reduction of the real interest rate by 8 percentage points.

As increased investment demand hits an economy with a lot of underutilized labour, its positive effects is translated directly into higher real output growth and higher real incomes. Moreover, the increase in investment, associated with the macroeconomic turn-around, was not only a short-run demand phenomenon, but also provided China's economy with the necessary savings to finance this investment. People's absolute savings increased with higher wages[11] but, more importantly, profits increased even more than overall income – with real wages, despite strong increases lagging behind productivity growth. Hence, companies initially created savings by retaining profits, which in turn could be used to finance surging investment during this period.

The Chinese approach of stabilizing a competitive exchange rate, which triggered export growth, stimulated capital accumulation and induced second round effects on wages and private consumption, is

---

[10] According to *World Business Environment Survey 2000*, the problem of obtaining finance, and especially long-term bank loans, is the most pressing issue for private business in China.

[11] Nevertheless, as a World Bank study of 2000 shows, the saving ratio of private households in China is rather normal and as low as 10 per cent throughout most of the 1990s (Kraay 2000).

Table 2
EMPIRICAL INVESTMENT FUNCTION

Dependent Variable: LINV
Method: Least Squares
Date: 04/14/04   Time: 16:05
Sample (adjusted): 1990 2003
Included observations: 14 after adjusting endpoints

Variable	Coefficient	Std. Error	t-Statistic	Prob.
C	-1.431585	0.904111	-1.583416	0.1478
R	-0.010904	0.001092	-9.982887	0.0000
LEX	0.476212	0.051449	9.256019	0.0000
LPC	0.627450	0.109262	5.742603	0.0003
DP95	0.083741	0.020490	4.087002	0.0027
R-squared	0.999234	Mean dependent var		14.00722
Adjusted R-squared	0.998893	S.D. dependent var		0.530379
S.E. of regression	0.017647	Akaike info criterion		-4.964018
Sum squared resid	0.002803	Schwarz criterion		-4.735783
Log likelihood	39.74813	F-statistic		2933.374
Durbin-Watson stat	2.081142	Prob (F-statistic)		0.000000

Variables	
C	Constant
R	Real interest rate (lending rate)
LEX	Log exports
LPC	Log private consumption
DP95	Dummy: 0 for 1990 to 1994; 1 for 1995 onwards

not a completely new approach. Williamson (1999) and UNCTAD (2003) highlighted this profit-investment nexus at work in other successful Asian economies such as Japan, the Republic of Korea and Taiwan Province of China. Rodrik (1996) and many others even attribute the so-called "German miracle", the rapid catch-up and rebuilding of Germany's economy after World War II, to such an exchange rate plus heterodox policy elements strategy.

II.2.   The role of the wage regime

Since 1994 the Chinese authorities have been able to combine an aggressive growth-orientated macroeconomic policy with a combination of a stable and competitive exchange rate, a low interest rate and low domestic inflation. In short, China has managed to implement a policy strategy of monetary laxity without losing control over its key monetary policy target of price stability. This strategy, we shall argue in this Section, was made possible by the new wage regime that the Chinese government introduced after 1994.

In light of the inflationary intermezzo before 1994, authorities realized the crucial importance of the stability (of the growth rate) of the domestic wage level. In fact, China's wage reform in 1994/1995 killed at least three birds with one stone: It helped control the inflation rate by linking wage development to productivity; it helped to keep the nominal exchange rate at a competitive level; and it further strengthened China's international position by very closely aligning nominal wage increases to productivity growth. This monetary environment created extraordinarily attractive conditions for domestic and foreign investors. Indeed, China's ability and willingness to control and to discourage short-term speculative capital flows have directly contributed to the attraction of long-term and fixed capital investments.[12]

Using the non-orthodox instrument of wage controls to fight inflation freed monetary policy from going after its traditional domestic target and stabilizing the nominal exchange rate. Despite a vigorously growing economy, inflationary pressure was kept at bay throughout the 1990s and accelerated only after 2002 when, in conjunction with a strong recovery of the world economy and soaring commodity prices, the Chinese economy approached a stage of overheating. Whereas the costs and benefits of the Chinese unilateral peg to the dollar have quickened interest in many countries and regions, the fact that the success of this approach was based on income policy has been overlooked by most observers.

II.2.1. Main features of the wage regimes in the reform period

China's wage regime in 1978 was characterized by a centrally regulated salary system that, among others, determined the wages according to regions, occupations, industries and sectors. The heart of the system was a classification scheme with more than 300 standardized occupational classifications used for salary formation.

---

[12] An empirical assessment of the amount of discouragement for short-term flows can be found in UNCTAD (2004).

After the beginning of the reform process in 1978 the wage regime underwent three sets of reforms in 1985, 1992 and 1994/1995, respectively.[13] This paper will mainly focus on the reform in 1994/1995. However, a short explanation of prior reforms helps to better understand the strategic role of the 1994/1995 reform.

The main and common feature of the two earlier reforms of 1985 and 1992 was a backward-looking indexation of wages to inflation. The 1985 reform, for instance, introduced profit-oriented factors as well as regional aspects to the wage-finding process. For example, the centrally planned budget dealing with the allocation of wages explicitly considered regional differences. The dynamics of the local consumer price index constituted an important regional factor, in addition to unemployment and regional growth rates. Later, in the reform of 1992, enterprises were given the authority to set wages according to their own needs by allowing them to relate discretionary wage setting to their individual economic performance and enabling enterprises to propose a wage budget based on their own calculations. These were then reviewed by the central authorities who took inflation and other local wages into account.[14] The important commonality of both reforms was the indexation of wages to the development of the consumer price index generating the well-known vicious circle of backward-looking indexation: a shock, affecting inflation, impacts the wage level, and rising nominal wages trigger a new round of inflationary acceleration.[15]

In light of the inflationary bout in 1994/1995, the authorities decided to de-couple nominal wages from the inflation rate. This attempt to break the vicious circle of accelerating inflation and rising inflation expectations was successful. The reform can be divided into a stricter rules-based part (1994/1995 I) and a more blurred recommendations-based part (1994/1995 II). Companies eligible to set their wages under the rules-based component could use their discretion within the framework of two standards: Firstly, the growth rate of the total salaries of an enterprise had to remain below the growth rate of after-tax profitability. Secondly, the growth rate of per-capita wages ought

---

[13] Cf. Yueh (2004), p. 151ff.

[14] Ibid.

[15] For a detailed discussion of the development of the inflation rate in China for the period of 1978 to 1995, please refer to Imai (1997).

to be less than the growth rate of labour productivity. Within the recommendation-based part of the reform, the "MOL [*Ministry of Labour*, the authors] suggested that enterprises should set wages not only in relation to occupation and rank, but also based on skills and [*individual*, the authors] productivity."[16]

Publicly listed companies on the Shanghai or Shenzhen stock exchange were eligible for the 1994/1995 I reform; however, a considerable proportion of publicly-listed companies are subject to state control. Thus, the scope and impact of the reforms depend on the Government's willingness and ability to enforce wage rules. Companies eligible for the 1994/1995 II reforms were those SOEs that underwent (in full or in part) an ownership-transformation without being listed on the stock exchange.[17] The number of companies and employees falling under the 1994/1995 II wage reform scheme was much higher than under the 1994/1995 I reform.

The two reform approaches differed in content and scope. The second part was a guideline rather than a strictly enforced regulation. Unfortunately, due to lack of data it is impossible to determine the proportion of those enterprises actually following the guideline. Particularly, the number of employees falling under the reform agenda at all is an open question. Nevertheless, the next Section provides a very rough assessment of both, the number of employees subject to the reforms as well as their income.

II.2.2. The scope of the wage reforms in the mid-1990s

A useful assessment of the impact of the wage reforms has to establish the scope of the reform measures in terms of the number of employees and their wage bill in relation to the total Chinese wage bill within the 1990s.[18] The share of the SOEs in the total wage bill has been falling rapidly in the last decade (Table 3).

---

[16] Yueh (2004), p. 153.

[17] Ibid.

[18] Even though the 1994/1995 I reform scheme affects state-owned as well as privately-owned companies, we have lumped them together as state-owned companies. This is justified by the fact that the share of purely private enterprises within the public listed companies is only between 16 and 35 per cent, and that the overall impact of the 1994/1995 I wage reform was very limited and the reported wage spread was only 8 per cent.

Table 3
THE SHARE OF STATE-OWNED INDUSTRIAL ENTERPRISES OF THE
TOTAL CHINESE WAGE BILL

Year	SOEs' employment (Million)	Average wage/year (RMB)	SOEs' wage bill (Million RMB)	Total wage bill (Million RMB)	SOEs' share of total wage bill (Per cent)
1991	44.72	2,477	110 771	332 390	33.33
1992	45.21	2,878	130 114	393 920	33.03
1993	44.98	3,532	158 869	491 620	32.32
1994	43.69	4,797	209 581	665 640	31.49
1995	**43.97**	**5,625**	**247 331**	**810 000**	**30.53**

Source: Authors' calculations based on *China Statistical Yearbook* (various issues) and Datastream.

State-owned units contributed around 33 per cent of all Chinese wages paid in 1991 and to 17 per cent in 2001. This declining share constitutes the upper limit of the wage reform's impact: If it is assumed that the wage reform had a guiding influence on all state-owned units in the industrial sector, it impacted on around a third of all the companies in 1995 and less than a fifth in 2001. However, as shown above, the wage reform did not apply to all state-owned units.

According to the China Securities and Regulatory Commission (CSRC) there have been 1,160 listed companies on China's stock exchanges in 2001. Out of this group, 415 had no state shares or no shares subscribed by the state, which accounts for one third of all listed companies.[19] As non state-controlled publicly-listed companies should welcome any increase in productivity-linked discretion in wage setting, we assume that all non-state companies and all state-controlled public companies adhered to the 1994/1995 I reform scheme.[20] In this case, the 1994/1995 I wage reform affected around 3 million employees with a wage of around RMB35 billion, representing 3 per cent of the total Chinese wage bill in 2001 (Table 4). The available data is insufficient to estimate the impact in

---

[19] China Internet Information Centre (2003); Qu (2003).
[20] The reported average wage level of state-owned units and non state-owned units in 2001 is rather similar at RMB11,178 and RMB12,140, i.e. we use the first wage level for the whole calculation.

1995. But, as there were considerably fewer companies falling under the 1994/1995 I wage scheme compared to 2001, one can assume that the influence in 1995 fell short of, or was up to 3 per cent.

Table 4
POTENTIAL SCOPE OF 1994/1995 I WAGE REFORM

Year	Companies	Average employment in sample	Projected employment (Million)	Listed companies' wage bill	Listed companies' share of total wage bill (Per cent)
1995	323	*(Insufficient data available)*			
2001	1,160	2,704	3.14	35,099	2.97

Source: Authors' calculations based on *China Statistical Yearbook* (various issues) and Datastream.

The evaluation of the 1994/1995 II wage reform is based on a much broader statistical coverage. In the mid-1990s around 40 per cent of SOEs could be classified as forming part of the so-called recommendation-based wage regime.[21] In 2001 around 65 per cent of all SOEs underwent an ownership transformation without being listed on one of the stock exchanges.[22] Based on these two figures, the effect of the 1994/1995 II wage reform, in terms of its impact in percentage of the total Chinese wage bill in 1995 and 2001, was considerable (Table 5).

In 1995 around 17.6 million employees were affected by the recommendation-based part of the wage reform and earned an average wage of RMB5,625 in 1995, which generated a wage bill of around RMB99 billion. Due to the serious concerns about the inflationary environment of the mid-1990s (discussed in more detail below) the potential scope of the wage reform was actually used. Thus, according to the 1994/1995 II wage reform, the authorities could directly influence RMB99 billion of wages. This constituted a share of 12.21 per cent of the total Chinese wage bill in 1995 and 11.20 per cent in 2001.

---

[21] Yueh (2004).
[22] China Internet Information Centre (2003).

Table 5
POTENTIAL SCOPE OF 1994/1995 II WAGE REFORM

Year	SOEs' employment (Million)	Average wage/year (RMB)	SOEs' wage bill (Million RMB)	1994/1995 II employment (Million)	1994/1995 II wage bill (Million RMB)	Total wage bill (Million RMB)	1994/1995 II share of total wage bill (Per cent)
1991	44.72	2,477	110 771	n.a.	n.a.	332 390	n.a.
1992	45.21	2,878	130 114	n.a.	n.a.	393 920	n.a.
1993	44.98	3,532	158 869	n.a.	n.a.	491 620	n.a.
1994	43.69	4,797	209 581	n.a.	n.a.	665 640	n.a.
1995	**43.97**	**5,625**	**247 331**	**17.59**	**98,933**	**810 000**	**12.21**
1996	42.78	6,280	268 658	n.a.	n.a.	908 000	n.a.
1997	40.40	6,747	272 579	n.a.	n.a.	940 530	n.a.
1998	27.21	7,668	208 646	n.a.	n.a.	929 650	n.a.
1999	24.12	8,543	206 057	n.a.	n.a.	987 550	n.a.
2000	20.96	9,552	200 210	n.a.	n.a.	1 065 620	n.a.
2001	**18.24**	**11,178**	**203 887**	**11.86**	**132,526**	**1 183 090**	**11.20**

Source: Authors' calculations based on *China Statistical Yearbook* (various issues) and Datastream.

PRICE CONTROLS AS A SECOND NON-MONETARY POLICY TOOL

Price controls were the second non-monetary policy tool used by the Chinese authorities to keep inflation low in the 1990s.

Even in the modern and transformed Chinese economy, three kinds of prices can be identified: [1]

(a) *Market-regulated prices,* which are set solely by market forces without any intervention of authorities.
(b) *Government guided prices,* which can come either as a benchmark price or a floating range set by the government. The floating band is usually between 5 and 15 per cent.
(c) *Government prices,* which are fixed prices set by the responsible government authorities and are changeable only through approval of this authority.

Article 26 of the Price Law of the People's Republic of China states that price controls are designed to influence the general price level. In the chapter on 'Control and Adjustment to General Price Level' the article states: "To stabilize the general price level is one of the major objectives of macro-economic policy." In the following articles the law leaves no doubt that price controls are considered as an instrument of macro-economic policy to influence the general price level.

Evidence exists of the government's active use of the tool of price controls in the post-WTO era as well. The recent threat of an overheating economy with growing inflation rates in 2004 prompted the authorities to employ price control measures more frequently again. Accordingly, controlling the prices can be directly or indirectly pursued, e.g.:

• The National Reform and Development Commission (NRDC) in China instructed provincial authorities in March 2004 to freeze any approval for price increases for the next quarter of the year. The freeze applies if either the m-o-m local CPI growth reaches 1 per cent or higher or y-o-y monthly local CPI reaches 4 per cent or higher for three consecutive months.[2]
• Using a more indirect measure, the NRDC also asked local governments to set ceilings for profit rates for fertilizer wholesales, e.g. 3 per cent in Heilongjiang and 2 per cent in Hunan Province. Additionally, a 50 per cent rebate on VAT in the fertilizer industry was re-introduced. The move was aimed at raising the output of crop and thus to reduce the inflationary prices in the food sector.[3]

These recent developments reflect similar discussions on more effective price controls during the high inflation period of 1993-1995. In June 1995 the China Daily published an article with the title "Strong measures need to guide pricing system".[4] article quotes a research fellow in a State Council research centre who pointed out that the lack of price controls in the market economy had a strong influence on the acceleration of inflation at that time. Subsequently, despite some success of traditional instruments to fight inflation, the Price Law of the People's Republic of China was introduced in 1998. Later on, the scope of the controls was incorporated in the legal framework produced to accompany Chinese WTO negotiations.

While there is no sign that the authorities want to re-introduce controls beyond the Price Law and the WTO agreement, it is evident that they use their discretion in setting price controls more actively in times of inflationary or deflationary pressure. In 1998, for instance, the first year of the deflationary period of the late 1990s, the authorities used the instrument and set minimum prices in 21 industries to ease the deflationary pressure.[5] However, the results were moderate as the deflationary environment lasted for four years.

It is a difficult, if not impossible task, to assess the exact impact of the price controls on China's rate of inflation. However, in a recent HSBC study Qu (2004) estimates that the effect of the price controls in the overheating economy in July 2004 kept the inflation rate on a level of almost half of the level without controls: "Without the government's controls over the prices of electricity, coal and transportation, both the producer price index (PPI) and the consumer price index (CPI) would have been rising at close to 10 per cent rather than the official July figures of 6.4 and 5.3 per cent, respectively."[6]

It is important to note a major macroeconomic downside of the instrument of price controls: If price controls prevent rising prices in an overheating economy, the automatic stabilizer of decreasing demand for certain products cannot play its role. Current reports about shortages in certain sectors and energy blackouts suggest that price controls in those sectors may have prevented the built-in stabilizer to work effectively.[7]

---

[1] According to the report of the working party on the accession of China into the World Trade Organization (WTO) of October 1, 2001.
[2] Cf. Wu (2004).
[3] Cf. People's Daily (2004); Tan (2004).
[4] Cf. Fu (1995).
[5] Cf Roberts (1998)
[6] Cf QU (2004) p. 5.
[7] Cf. Areddy (2004); Qu (2004), p. 5.

To summarize, both reforms may have impacted between 12 and 15 per cent of the total wage bill in 1995 and around 14 per cent in 2001.

II.2.3. The Macroeconomic effects of the 1994/1995 wage reform

In China, as elsewhere, nominal unit labour cost growth (ULC)[23] is one of the most important determinants of the inflation rate. The growth of nominal wages in relation to productivity is decisive for the inflation rate, as the overall domestic cost level in a vertically-integrated economy more or less exclusively consists of labour inputs in different forms. Figure 10 shows the close links between unit labour cost changes and the inflation rate. Thus the authorities were able to set an upper limit for inflation through the control of nominal wages – the objective of the wage reform – that would only be in danger to be perforated if the demand-pull effect in the economy would dominate the cost-push component. However, since the beginning of the reform this has not been the case.

Figure 10
UNIT LABOUR COST GROWTH AND INFLATION RATE, 1987–2000

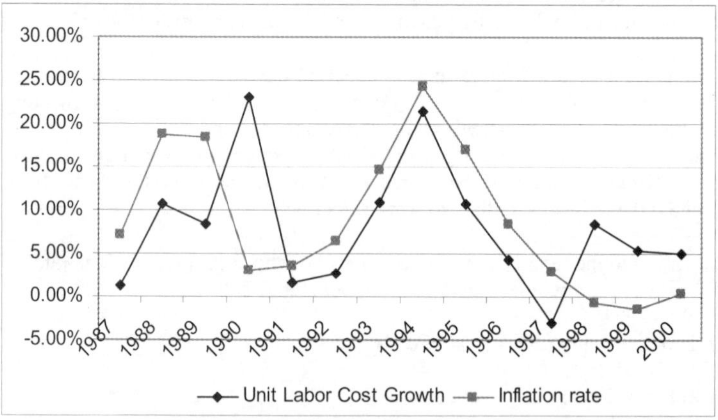

Source: Authors' calculation based on ILO, *Laborsta Internet Database* and IMF, *International Financial Statistic.*

---

[23] Change rate of gross income of employed population divided by the real GDP in RMB.

Whereas in the late 1980s and the early 1990s the growth rate of unit labour was volatile and high, in the aftermath of the reforms of 1994, volatility and growth of this important cost component was brought under control. The last inflationary bout of 25 per cent in 1994 marked the end of the old era of macroeconomic stabilization. In subsequent years unit labour cost growth fell to 4.37 per cent in 1996 and to -3.03 per cent in 1997. The inflation rate mirrored this development with 8.32 and 2.81 per cent in 1996 and 1997, respectively. In 1997 and 1998 unit labour cost and nominal wage growth jumped by almost 10 per cent again, well above the inflation rate.

From 1998 onwards deflationary pressure was a main feature of the Chinese economy with real wages making good on some of the income losses that labour had suffered from in previous years. The de-coupling of the inflation rate from the development of the unit labour costs and the implied de-coupling of the real wage from productivity may reflect the growing scarcity of labour after twenty years of vigorous growth (Figure 11). Additionally, the end of the

Figure 11
REAL WAGE AND PRODUCTIVITY GROWTH, 1987–2000

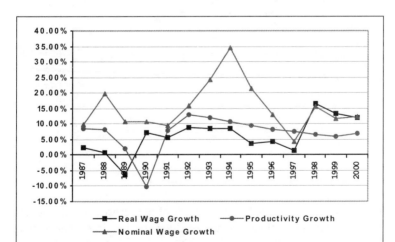

Source: Authors' calculation based on ILO, *Laborsta Internet Database* and IMF, *International Financial Statistics.*

slowdown of real wage growth in 1997 marks the return to a phase of a briskly growing Chinese economy without facing the inflationary difficulties of the early 1990s. In 1997 real wage growth had fallen to 1.34 per cent, this was before the effects of the wage reform on nominal wages faded successively.

Overall, the wage reform was a success. Obviously, despite the absence of government instruments to enforce strict adherence to the reform, the majority of companies that were eligible for the recommendation-based wage reform 1994/1995 II actually incorporated skill- and productivity-levels into the factors deter-mining wage-setting decision.

Nevertheless, the overall pattern of wage development was strongly influenced by the economic cycle (Figure 12).

Figure 12
THE ECONOMIC CYCLE AND THE WAGE DEVELOPMENT

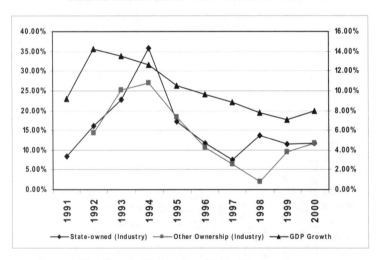

Source: China Statistical Yearbook, various issues

One of the main reasons for the success of the reform was the general unease about the inflation that prevailed at the time. The official inflation rate in 1994 had reached 24 per cent. At the same time, unemployment was rising due to growing numbers of migrant workers and accelerating lay-offs in SOEs.[24] The mix of social insecurity and high inflation rates led to increasing incidents of social unrest in the mid-1990s. According to a poll conducted by the Chinese Academy of Social Sciences and the National Statistical Bureau of China, 84 per cent of those polled found inflation to be the main reason for people being unsatisfied.[25] For the Government the situation must have been comparable with 1988/1989 when rising unemployment of state-owned workers, stagnating social benefits and high inflation rates of between 10 and 20 per cent led to noticeable social unrest.[26] As an observer put it: "One explanation why workers joined the huge demonstrations that China saw in 1989 ... is unhappiness over inflation."[27] In 1994 the situation was just as serious, and the government authorities were looking for a means to fight inflation that would not magnify the unemployment problem.[28] It must have been due to that constellation that the choice was made to use non-monetary instruments to tackle inflation and to fix the exchange rate at a competitive level to avoid dependence on the international capital market.

II.3. Complementary macroeconomic management

II.3.1. The role of fiscal policy

The basic stability of the Chinese economy since 1994 was mainly the result of the stable and pro-growth monetary environment. However, there were other policies that assisted monetary and exchange rate policy. The most important element supporting the remarkable stability of the rate of growth and inflation in China was the efficient and prudent use of fiscal demand management. As the traditional instrument of monetary policy, the short-term interest rate was not available, due to the unilateral fixing of the exchange rate, a larger burden of adjustment had to be borne by fiscal policy.

---

[24] Zhang (1995).
[25] Cheng (1995).
[26] Wang (2002).
[27] Areddy (2004).
[28] The negative inflation bias of Chinese decision-makers may be due to their experience with the period of hyper-inflation in the second half of the 1940s (Burdekin et al., 2001, p. 4).

The active cooling down of the economy in 1994/1995 represents a good example of the effective use of budgetary tools. Investment at the time was growing rapidly and was fuelling inflationary risks. Consumer price inflation had accelerated from 3.5 per cent in 1991 to 14.5 per cent in 1993 and climbed to 24 per cent in 1994. Despite a hike in bank lending rates – increased from 8.6 per cent in 1991 to 12 per cent in 1995 – the acceleration of inflation overcompensated the increase in the nominal rates and real interest rates fell. Although the central bank restricted lending requirements, it withdrew refinancing credits and reduced special-project loans (Lin and Schramm 2003), fiscal policies were introduced to cool the boom.

Government expenditure in infrastructure investment was signifi-cantly driven down to rein in the boom.[29] Figure 13 also displays the development of SOEs' investments and shows that the

Figure 13
CHANGE IN GOVERNMENT AND SOE INVESTMENT, 1991–2002

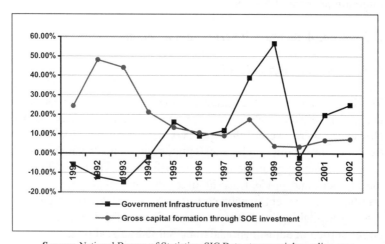

Source: National Bureau of Statistics; SIC Data at www.xinhuaonline.com.

---

[29] Unlike in a more marketized economy, the Government's budget deficit is not necessarily the best indicator for fiscal policy in China. This is due to the fact that a vast array of policy goals is pursued by using the lever of SOEs' investment and employment changes. Thus, the Government's actual budgetary expenses traditionally only represent a relatively small share of GDP (11.5 per cent in 2002) with a much higher share hidden in SOE budgets.

growth rates declined significantly from 1992 to 1994. It is obvious that the Government used SOE investment expenditures to influence the business cycle too. Thus, Chinese fiscal policies disposed of a substantive leverage through the interaction of official governmental and SOE expenditures.

By contrast, in the wake of the Asian crisis of 1997/1998, the Government used active fiscal policy to increase demand. With important trading partners and competitors being forced to devalue their currencies and to restrict overall expenditure, China was hit by an adverse demand shock, mostly in manufacturing. Within one year roughly 10 per cent of the workforce in the manufacturing sector was laid off. Economic policy reacted strongly and quickly. Interest rates were sharply cut, the bank rate fell from 8.6 per cent in 1997 to 3.2 per cent in 1999 and the lending rate from 8.6 to 5.9 per cent, but the strongest anti-cyclical effect stemmed from fiscal policy. Government investment in infrastructure rose by 38.9 per cent in 1998 and by an additional 56.5 per cent in 1999 (Figure 13). Investments among SOEs also increased. From 1997 to 1998 the growth rate increased from 9 to 17.4 per cent. However, compared to the early 1990s the impact of SOE's investment diminished because growth rates again decreased to 3.8 per cent in 1999. This reflects the decreasing economic weight of SOEs as market reforms took hold in the course of the 1990s.

II.3.2. The role of industrial policy and deregulation

The macroeconomic policy of the 1990s was flanked by specific industrial policy and deregulation measures. Some of these measures were explicitly designed to promote exports, encourage foreign investment and to develop relative advantages in some manufacturing sectors. The end of the dual exchange rate regime and the unification of the official and the swap exchange rate in 1994 were of particular importance in the promotion of exports as it removed what had in effect been a tax on exports. Before the reform, exporters had to hand over a certain part of their foreign exchange revenue at the official exchange rate, which was above the swap rate. Thus, they were subsidizing state-owned importers, which could obtain foreign exchange at the official rate (Lin and Schramm 2003). The reform stopped these implicit and costly subsidies and hence promoted exports.

In addition to this the Government intervened heavily in favour of certain export industries. To this end, the Chinese authorities used various industrial policy instruments. For example, all levels of governments were allowed to use direct financial support for key industries. Also, different taxes and levies were imposed on different activities. In the early 1990s, for example, a tax was levied on domestic enterprises conducting investment businesses. The "Coordination Tax for Directions of Fixed Capital Investment" was introduced in 1991 and represented a surcharge on investment varying from 0 to 30 per cent, depending on project categories and the state industrial policy. In addition, the tax burden varied by industry due to different charges levied for city maintenance and construction, consumption tax, resource tax and education. According to Lu (2000), in the late 1990s these charges ranged from an implicit sales tax level of roughly 20 per cent for manufacturers in electronic and telecommunication equipment to 77 per cent for petroleum processing and coke refinery.

In retrospect, the attempts of Chinese authorities to foster certain industries over others have not ended up in hopelessly distorted production structures. Many of those sectors which benefited from lower tax burdens, e.g. companies manufacturing office machinery, instruments, electronic and telecommunication equipment as well as ordinary machinery, appear to have been particularly successful in terms of export performance in the last decade.

Foreign enterprises played a special role in this strategy. They were attracted in the hope of delivering know-how in technology-intensive sectors and in access to world markets. To attract the desired companies, in 1986 the authorities divided foreign activities into three different classes: (a) Those that should be encouraged; (b) those that should be tolerated; and (c) those that should be banned. Activities in the export sector and in high-technology sectors were especially favoured. Thus, foreign-owned enterprises active in these sectors received various benefits such as tax obligations, credit access, input charges, labour management and export rights (Huang 2003). The special treatment of favourable FDI meant that some foreign companies received more substantial guarantees than domestically-owned private companies. For example, the Chinese Government made a constitutional commitment in 1982 not to nationalize or expropriate the assets of foreign investors without "due cause and compensation". For domestically-owned property, in contrast, a similar proposition was only added into the constitution in March 2004. Huang (2003) shows that in the manufacturing industry, including electronics and machinery, but excluding the automobile industry, foreign companies have to pay significantly lower local government taxes than domestic private firms. Moreover, the author also finds indications that foreign-owned firms are treated more favourably than domestic private firms in terms of public auditing standards, as well as within the judiciary system. Accordingly, this special treatment has led to significant better export performance of foreign companies compared to domestic enterprises. Paradoxically, the combination of an open foreign sector with a skeptical attitude towards domestic private activities eventually led to a better business environment for foreign than for the Chinese enterprises.

III. THE ROLE OF FDI

Many elements of China's growth experience have been similar to those of other Asian countries, but the strong reliance on foreign direct investment in China has been quite distinct.[30] While none of the other countries concerned had large inflows of FDIs during their strong growth-periods,[31] foreign direct investment to China averaged 4.9 per cent of GDP from 1991 to 2002.

Meanwhile, according to Lemoine (2000), foreign-owned enterprises have gained a decisive role in China's export sector. At present more than half of the country's exports come from foreign owned firms, and the share is still rising (Figure 14). Additionally, since the beginning of the 1990s FDI has gained ever-growing importance in China's domestic economy. Between 1991 and 1994 the share of FDI in the country's gross fixed capital formation increased from 3.9 to more than 17 per cent.[32] Over the same time, its share in GDP grew from 1.5 to 6.7 per cent.

---

[30] Various issues of UNCTAD *World Investment Report* (WIR), in particular WIR 2001.

[31] Though detailed FDI data for Japan is not available, it is well known that the Japanese economy was rather closed during the period from 1961 to 1973 and FDI almost non-existent (Werner 2003).

[32] FDI does not transmit one-to-one into fixed capital formation as in some cases only the ownership of assets is transferred. However, the indicator gives an impression of the importance of FDI relative to overall investment.

Figure 14
EXPORT SHARE GENERATED BY FOREIGN-OWNED-FIRMS

Source: Ministry of Commerce of China.

In recent years, the relative importance of FDI has decreased. In 2002 real GDP has increased by roughly 90 per cent over 1994, while annual FDI inflow deflated with the investment deflator increased by "only" 40 per cent, which is still a significant rise, but clearly below GDP growth rates. However, the decline in the share of FDI in overall gross fixed capital formation understates the importance of foreign enterprises in some sectors: Foreign investors still carry out more than 20 per cent of all non-government and non-SOE investments. Finally, FDI stocks account for a significant share of the domestic capital stock. UNCTAD estimates that foreign companies own roughly 14 per cent of the capital stock.[33]

The policy approach behind the FDI boom is often described as the Chinese "open door policy", which entails actively encouraging foreign companies to invest in China. The rationale behind the policy

---

[33] The number is derived as follows: Inward FDI stock in dollars is converted into 1990 Yuan using the investment deflator. This number is set into relation to an estimated capital stock using the perpetual inventory methods from Chinese investment data going back to the 1960s. While this way might not be the most accurate method, given the large technological changes in China's investment during the past decade, it seems to be the best proxy available.

is the Government's hope to induce a leap-frog of the technological base. This policy has to be clearly distinguished from the approaches chosen earlier in Japan or the Republic of Korea, where active industrial policy in the development periods of the 1950s–1970s tried to build national champions that could compete technologically in certain sectors on world markets.

IV. POLICY CONCLUSIONS

China's experience in the past decade can be seen as a model of a successful development strategy. As in other Asian countries in the past, fixing the real exchange rate at a favourable level and promoting exports offers the possibility of penetrating world markets rapidly and experiencing strong growth and capital accumulation. The penetration of foreign markets brings about the rise in income needed to finance increased investment without recourse to net foreign capital inflows. However, such a strategy is not easy to put into practice, as there are a number of interacting elements to observe.

First, nominal wage increases have to be kept under control in order to maintain the overall favourable competitive position. If it is not possible to keep wage increases in line with productivity (in comparison with the most important trading partners), a crawling peg with a constant devaluation compensating for inflationary wage increases might be the second best solution. However, managing a constant slow depreciation and a constant exchange rate, are not easy to pursue with a completely open capital account (UNCTAD 2004). Volatile private capital flows induced by interest rate differentials or the expectation of exchange rate changes can force the central bank to intervene heavily and to find unorthodox ways to avoid overheating of the economy. Thus, capital controls might be unavoidable in such a strategy at a certain point of time.

Second, to use domestic macroeconomic tools such as monetary and fiscal policy to keep the domestic economy from overheating and thus wages from overshooting, a comfortable surplus in the current account is an asset.[34] Deficits in the current account increase the dependence on foreign capital inflows and interest rate terms in international markets. Uncontrolled private capital inflows threaten to amplify booms even more than central bank intervention, thereby endangering the control of domestic monetary developments. Moreover, if volatile private capital flows reverse suddenly, restrictive macroeconomic tools need to be used to bring domestic demand down to the level at which the current account adjusts. Such a stop-and-start macroeconomic policy not only lowers welfare directly, but also reduces the incentive for long-term investment and thus dampens capital accumulation and long-term growth prospects.

One imminent problem for China might be a shift in the predominant type of FDI. While a large part of FDI hitherto used to be of the efficiency-seeking kind and targeted at the export sector, FDI can be expected to become increasingly market-seeking in the future. First, with the recent trend towards a slow real appreciation of the Renminbi, purchasing power in foreign currencies will increase and thus market opportunities in China will improve while efficiency-seeking investment in manufactures for export will become less attractive. Second, WTO accession gives foreign firms access to service sectors such as finance. Investment in these sectors will, by definition, be market-seeking.

This shift in FDI might pose problems for China. Different from efficiency-seeking FDI, which has actually helped China gain access to world markets and thus to earn foreign exchange, market-seeking FDI probably leads to profit repatriation later on, which might translate in the outflow of foreign exchange and burden the current account of the balance of payments. In order to minimize the negative impact of this shift in the structure of FDI, the capacities of domestic firms to successfully compete against the new market entrants need to be strengthened.

---

[34] At first sight, one might believe that an undervalued currency cannot be observed at the same time as a current account deficit. However, this does not necessarily have to be true as the current account deficit can also stem from structural reasons (such as inelastic demand for some import commodity or a structural outflow of profit remittances).

Central to this goal seems to be the removal of legal and administrative discrimination against domestic private firms relative to foreign owned companies as described by Huang (2003). It may be helpful to enable easier access to bank credit which, to a large extent, seems to be targeted toward SOEs. According to the *World Bank Business Environment Survey 2000*, access to finance is the single most important obstacle to doing business in China. Almost half of those private Chinese firms surveyed complain about the lack of access to long term bank loans. Attempts to strengthen market-oriented loan allocation among banks might help to alleviate this problem.

Both of these steps would have the potential to improve the export performance of privately-owned domestic Chinese firms. While investment of domestic private firms is booming, their exports are growing much slower than those of foreign owned companies. With a removal of the discrimination, they might find the possibility to enhance their share of export markets. As for privately-owned domestic firms compared to partly or completely foreign-owned firms, this would also help to stabilize the surplus in the current account.

Another imminent issue is the need to improve macroeconomic management. As described above, with a shrinking weight of SOEs in total employment and therefore in the determination of overall wages and prices and an increasingly open (or porous) capital account, a larger weight to stabilize the economy (and the price level) should be placed on fiscal policy. Restrictive fiscal policy has the potential to slow a boom and dampen inflation without inducing new capital inflows. This might even become more important for China with the increasing operation of foreign banks after the WTO accession and the gradual liberalization of capital inflows.

In China, however, there have been signs that centrally controlling fiscal policy (and especially the investment of SOEs) has become a problem of late. It is to be feared this might lead to an overheating of the economy and present a danger to the exchange rate regime in the medium term. In the 2003/2004 boom, the Central Government has to an increasing degree been unable to slow the growth in investment. One problem seems to be that central and local governments often do not work hand in hand towards a common objective. While the Central Government is well aware of the need to slow the economy, local governments seem to be reluctant to slow investments in their respective regions as they try to maintain high growth and employment. They even, to a certain extent, appear to counteract attempts by the Central Government to macro-manage the economy by encouraging local firms to increase investment despite the threats of an overheating economy.

Thus, if the current low real exchange set-up is to be sustainable, China needs to get better control over local government spending and local government-induced SOE investment. Tackling this problem would potentially help to alleviate other problems as well: There has been ample anecdotal evidence that a lot of parallel construction of capacities has been taking place, e. g. in the steel and aluminum sector as each provincial government has pushed the corresponding industry in its province into additional investment and encouraged banks to provide the necessary loans. A more centralized control over SOE capacity built-up and investment volumes (not microeconomic investment details) might help to reduce overlapping construction, the danger of a future fall of profitability in these sectors as well as the creation of new non-performing loans.

REFERENCES

Abel AB (1983). Optimal investment under uncertainty. *American Economic Review*, 73:228–233.

Agosin MR and Mayer R (2000). Foreign investment in developing countries. Does it crowd in domestic investment? *UNCTAD Discussion Paper,* No. 146. Geneva, United Nations Conference on Trade and Development, February.

Anderson J (2003). The complete RMB handbook. In: Asian *Economic Perspective*, UBS Investment Research, Hong Kong (China).

Areddy JT (2004). China's inflation weapon: price controls beat rising interest rates, but shortages result. In: *Wall Street Journal*, 20 August, New York.

Bayoumi T, Coe DT, and Helpman E (1999). R&D spillover and global growth. *Journal of International Economics*, 47:399–428.

Burdekin R and Whited Hsin-hui IH (2001). Exporting Hyperinflation: The Long Arm of Chiang Kai-shek. *Claremont Colleges Working Papers*, 2001-18. Claremont, CA, Claremont Colleges.

Chen Hongyi (2000). Institutional transition of China's township and village enterprises, market liberalization: conceptual form innovation and privatization. Studies on the Economic Reform of China. Aldershot, Hampshire: Ashgate Publishing Limited.

Cheng E (1996). Widespread protest alarm Beijing. *Green Left Weekly*, Issue 207, 18 October 1995, Chippendale, NSW.

Cheung KY and Lin P (2004). Spillover effects of FDI on innovation in China: Evidence from the provincial data. *China Economic Review*, 15:25–44.

China Internet Information Center (2003). Marketization of State-Owned Enterprises. In: http://www.china.org.cn, Beijing.

Chu WL (2000). Exchange rate variability and China's exports. *Journal of Comparative Economics*, 28:61–79.

Coady DP and Limin Wang (2000). Equity, efficiency, and labour-market reforms in urban China: the impact of bonus wages on the distribution of earnings. *China Economic Review*, 11:213–231.

Dixit A and Pindyck RS (1994). *Investment under Uncertainty*. Princeton, Princeton University Press.

Dullien S (2004). China's changing competitive position: lessons from a unit-labour-cost-based REER. Mimeo.

Dunning JH (1998). Globalization and the new geography of foreign direct investment. *Oxford Development Studies*, 26:47–70.

Fan EX (2003). Technological spillovers from foreign direct investment – a survey. *Asian Development Review*, 20:34–56.

Flassbeck H (2004). Saving, investment, debt and the transfer problem. Mimeo.

Fu Jian (1995). Strong measures needed to guide pricing system. In: *China Daily* (North American ed.), New York.

Hong W (1998). Financing export-oriented catching-up in Korea: credit-rationing, sustained high growth and financial chaos. *International Economic Journal*, 12 (1):141–153.

Huang Y (2003). One country, two systems: foreign-invested enterprises and domestic firms in China. *China Economic Review*, 14:404–416.

Imai Hiroyuki (1997). Output-inflation tradeoff in China. In: *The Developing Economies*, 35(2):111–141, Chiba.

IMF (2004). Competitors will have to adjust as China continues to grow. *IMF Survey*, 31 May 2004, 153–154.

Keidel A (2001). China's GDP expenditure accounts. *China Economic Review*, 12:355–367.

Keynes JM (1930). A treatise on money – the pure theory of money. In: *The Collected Writings of John Maynard Keynes*, Volume V, London and Basingstoke, Macmillan, 1973.

Kokko A (1994). Technology, market characteristics, and spillovers. *Journal of Development Economics*, 43:279–293.

Kraay A (2000). Household saving in China. In: *World Bank Economic Review*, September 2000, Washington DC.

Larraín G (1999). Industrialization and the optimal real exchange rate policy for an emerging economy. In: Collignon S, Pisani-Ferry J and Park YC, eds., *Exchange Rate Policies in Emerging Asian Countries*, 149–184. London, Routledge.

Lemoine F (2000). FDI and the opening up of China's economy. *CEPII Working Paper*, No. 2000-11, Paris.

Lemoine F and Ünal-Kesenci D (2002). China in the international segmentation of production process. *CEPII Working Paper*, No. 2002-02, Paris.

Lin G and Schramm RM (2003). China's foreign exchange policies since 1979: A review of developments and an assessment. *China Economic Review*, 14:246–280.

Liu X, Song H, Wei Y and Romilly P (1997). Country characteristics and foreign direct investment in China: a panel data analysis. *Weltwirtschaftliches Archiv*, 133(2):313–329.

Lu D (2000). Industrial policy and resource allocation: implications on China's participation in globalization. *China Economic Review*, 11:342–360.

Nair-Reichert U and Weinhold D (2001). Causality tests for cross-country panels: a new look at FDI and economic growth in developing countries. *Oxford Bulletin of Economic and Statistics*, 63(2)153–171.

Naughton B (1999). Reform einer Planwirtschaft: Ist China einzigartig?, In: Herr H and Hübner K, eds., *Der "lange Marsch" in die Marktwirtschaft. Entwicklungen und Erfahrungen in der VR China und Osteuropa*, Berlin, 45–76.

Ng F and Yeats A (2003). Major trade trends in East Asia. What are their implications for regional cooperation and growth? *World Bank Policy Research Working Paper*, 3084.

Nunnenkamp P and Spatz J (2003). Foreign direct investment and economic growth in developing countries: how relevant are host-country and industry characteristics? *Kiel Working Paper*, No. 1176.

People's Daily (2004). China takes measures to curb price rise. In: http://english.people.com.cn/, Beijing.

Qu Hongbin (2004). Still too hot. In: *China Economic Insight*, Volume 17. The Hong Kong and Shanghai Banking Corporation Ltd, Economic and Investment Strategy Unit, Hong Kong (China).

Qu Qiang (2003). Corporate governance and state-owned shares in China listed companies. In: *Journal of Asian Economics*, Volume 14:771–783, Stamford and Connecticut.

Roberts D (1998). So much for competition. Beijing slaps on price controls to stanch deflation. In: *Business Week*, Iss. 3606, New York.

Rodrik D (1995). Trade strategy, investment and exports. Another look at East Asia, *NBER Working Paper, 5339.*

Rodrik D (1996). Coordination failures and government policy: A model with application to East Asia and Eastern Europe, *Journal of International Economics*, 40:1–22.

Ros J (2000). *Development Theory and the Economics of Growth*, Ann Arbor, The University of Michigan Press.

Rumbaugh T and Blancher N (2004). China: International trade and WTO accession. *IMF Working Paper*, 04/36.

Sachs J and Wing Thye Woo (1997). Understanding China's economic performance. *NBER Working Paper*, 5935.

Servén L (2002). Real exchange rate uncertainty and private investment in developing countries. *Review of Economics and Statistics*, forthcoming.

Tan F (2004). China moves to curb high domestic fertiliser prices. In: *Asian Chemical News*, Volume 10, Iss. 442, Sutton.

Tinggui C (2001). The People's Bank of China and its monetary policy. *FHW Working Paper*, No. 14, Business Institute Berlin.

UNCTAD (2001). *World Investment Report 2001: Promoting Linkages.*. United Nations publication, Sales No. E.01.II.D.12, New York and Geneva.

UNCTAD (2003). *Trade and Development Report, 2003*. United Nations publication, Sales No. E.03.II.D.7, New York and Geneva.

UNCTAD (2004). *Trade and Development Report, 2004*. United Nations publication, Sales No. E. 04.II.D.29, New York and Geneva.

Wang Hui (2002). Unequal shares: how Tiananmen protests led to the new market economy. In: *Le Monde Diplomatique* (English edition), April 2002, Paris.

Werner R (2003). *Princes of the Yen: Japan's Central Bankers and the Transformation of the Economy*, New York, M.E. Sharpe.

Williamson J (1999). Discussion on: Industrialization and the optimal real exchange rate policy for an emerging economy. In: S Collignon S, Pisani-Ferry J and Park YC, eds., *Exchange Rate Policies in Emerging Asian Countries*, 185–186. London, Routledge.

World Bank (1997). *China 2020 – Development Challenges in the New Century*. Washington DC.

World Bank (2000). *World Bank Business Environment Survey 2000*. Washington DC.

World Bank (2005). *World Development Indicators Online*. Washington DC.

WTO (2004). World *Trade 2004: Stronger Than Expected Growth Spurs Modest Trade Recovery*, April 5. Geneva, World Trade Organization.

Wu Zhong (2004). Beijing orders price controls. In: http://www.thestandard.com.hk, Hong Kong.

Yueh LY (2004). Wage reforms in China during the 1990s. *Asian Economic Journal*, 18(2).

Zhang Kai (1995). Unemployment in China is worsening. *October Review*, 22(4), Hong Kong.

Zhang Q and Felmingham B (2001). The Relationship between inward direct foreign investment and China's provincial export trade. *China Economic Review*, 12:82–99.

GLOBALIZATION AND THE INTEGRATION OF CHINA INTO THE WORLD ECONOMY

Yuanjiang Sun

A SUMMARY OF THE PRESENTATION

A new feature of the recent globalization drive is the wider involvement of people and economies in global economic exchange. Additionally, economic actions are no longer limited to national economies and regions but can – and are even obliged to – cover global markets as well. Both these factors, i.e. wider involvement and wider coverage, mean that the changing influence of globalization on businesses and economies is now stronger than ever.

Due to its complexity, interpretations on globalization are manifold. Globalization is an ever-evolving concept that changes shape and the shape of the world. Accordingly, assessments of globalization are subjective, different and divided into negative and positive evaluations. Thus, globalization cannot act as a panacea for world development.

The future of globalization will be characterized by ever-increasing globalized trade and financial markets. All this will lead to the rising importance of transnational corporations and banks. Thus, globalization will, on the one hand establish its own inherent new rules and, on the other demand for the establishment of an international regulative framework. In achieving the establishment of a rules-based global economy, globalization will finally lead to a more effective participation of all players of the global markets.

China's integration into the global economy began with its open door policy in the late-1970s and early-1980s under the regime of Deng Xiaoping. Since then, China has step-by-step approached its target of a socialist market economy. The culmination of China's transition and integration into the world economy was reached with China's accession to the WTO in 2001.

China's gains and outcomes from globalization are manifold. Supported by a more active Chinese role in regional economic cooperation, China ranked third in world exports and fourth in world imports with a trade volume of US$620.7 billion in 2002 and more than US$800 billion in 2003. China received US$52.7 billion in FDI in 2002, making it the world's most important recipient of FDI in total terms. Moreover, China's investors increasingly go abroad and integrate themselves into the world economy with 2,382 enterprises in 128 countries and regions and a total investment of US$29.9 billion in 2002.

The positive outcome arising from China's integration is due to its successful use of emerging opportunities. These opportunities are mainly triggered by the readjustment of the industrial structure of developed countries and newly industrializing economies and their trend towards relocating labour-intensive industries. China was able to attract these industries by providing a stable and reliable policy environment and at the same time promoting innovative reforms. Moreover, through this, China could establish a mutual beneficial environment for international and national investors and an ever-rising standard of living for its own population.

There are challenges ahead. On the international level these challenges culminate in the increasing vacuum of insufficient rules in the global trade and financial system. On the national level the main challenge for China lies in the ever-increasing disparity of economic wealth and the unequal participation in economic growth. A closer cooperation between UNCTAD and the People's Republic of China will thus contribute to a better understanding of the challenges of globalization and its implications for China's development strategy.

CHINA AND ITS NEIGHBOURS: PARTNERS OR COMPETITORS FOR TRADE AND INVESTMENT?

John Weiss[1]

INTRODUCTION

The very rapid economic growth of China, its dramatic success in world export markets and its heavy receipts of foreign direct investment (FDI) have generated much thought and debate in policy and business circles in different parts of the world. From Malaysia to Mexico and from Indonesia to India the simple "threat or opportunity" question has been posed in relation to the "rise of China". Given the impact of geography on trade and investment patterns, such concerns have been greatest amongst China's most immediate neighbours. This paper examines the evidence from a number of recent empirical studies that address different aspects of this issue in the context of China's economic relations with East and Southeast Asian nations. The broad consensus is that whilst there may be risks to individual sectors in all countries concerned, the pattern of regional trade and investment that is emerging is mutually beneficial, provided enterprises and governments in China's regional partners respond effectively to the adjustments required.

This paper is organized as follows. The remainder of the introduction sketches out briefly some of the conceptual issues. The second section illustrates the differing trade structures between China and its regional partners, since the degree of complementarity is critical to the potential gains from expanded trade. The third section examines evidence on changes in export market share in third-country markets to assess the extent to which regional partners are losing market share to Chinese exports. The fourth section examines the FDI diversion argument. The fifth section looks at the potential benefits to the

[1] This paper draws principally on research by ADB Institute staff and Visiting Fellows conducted over the last two years. Any errors of interpretation are the responsibility of the author. The opinions expressed in this paper are those of the author and do not necessarily reflect the views of UNCTAD.

region (and to China itself) from various forms of trade liberalization arrangements. The final section draws some brief conclusions.

The "stylized fact" view of China is of a large, very rapidly growing economy with very high domestic savings, attracting large absolute values of FDI (but not, it should be noted, in per capita terms) and achieving dramatic export growth (averaging nearly 17 per cent annually 1990–2002). With a large rural population as a source of labour supply China's "modern sector" growth is seen as based on a near perfectly elastic labour supply at a low real wage based on low rural opportunity costs (a contemporary version of the "Lewis model" for a labour surplus economy). Given its size China thus becomes the marginal supplier for labour-intensive goods on the world market, and its real wage level and productivity set world prices in these products. FDI inflows and domestic investment in skills and technology upgrading allow a shift into more technologically sophisticated product ranges, particularly where labour-intensive segments of international supply chains can be relocated to China through FDI (although China lags well behind the Republic of Korea and Taiwan Province of China in technology indicators such as enterprise R&D expenditure per capita).

Falling trade costs (e.g. import tariffs, transport and freight charges, time in transit, the cost of information and managing international supply chains) have facilitated rapid regional integration in trade and capital flows within the East and Southeast Asian region. In addition to this, China's rapid expansion provides an opportunity for regional partners to export to and invest in its large domestic market. However, China is also an export rival in third-country markets (and a country's own domestic market) in a range of goods from simple labour-intensive products to the more technologically complex (for the latter principally because of its large FDI sector). If FDI to the region is treated as a fixed sum, then higher inflows to China will be at the expense of other economies and there will be FDI diversion as an additional possible negative effect that will have consequences for trade flows.

The competitive "threat" from China for particular goods can be seen in terms of changes in domestic market share (negative import substitution) and third-country markets. However whether rising international competition leads to income and welfare losses will depend upon the flexibility of economies. In a world of zero adjustment costs economies will simply adapt to changing relative costs and if market share is lost in one product, resources will shift into another where market prospects and returns are higher. The familiar argument which states that only firms, not nations, compete rests on a set of simplifying assumptions related to perfect markets and hence zero adjustment costs. In other words, with positive adjustment costs trade competition need not always be mutually beneficial for all different parties.

The impact of "the rise of China" and falling trade costs more generally can be thought of in simple terms of "trade diversion" and "trade creation". For any one economy, trade diversion arises where lower cost or higher quality goods (for example from China) displace those of the economy concerned, creating a potential loss of income if new markets are not found and the resources involved are not shifted to other activities. Trade creation is where growth elsewhere (for example in China) creates a demand for an economy's exports.[2] It will make a difference what type of products are the subject of this diversion and creation process. In general it is desirable for economies to shift up the "ladder of comparative advantage" that runs from simple labour-intensive goods, through capital-intensive, to human capital-intensive technologically sophisticated products. How this process is affected by closer trade links with a large fast growing regional neighbour will clearly be important and the dynamic implications of any new regional division of labour will matter. If an economy adapts by specializing in products with a static global market or a lack of technological dynamism, this new specialization pattern may offer lower growth prospects than the initial pre-adjustment one. A priori it is expected that the more adaptable are the firms in an economy, the greater is the scope for mutually beneficial outcomes from closer trade links. Also the greater is the scope for complementarity between partner economies, in terms of resource and human capital endowments, the greater the potential for trade creation and thus the greater will be the gains.[3]

---

[2] It should be noted that these are not the classic "Viner definitions" from the theory of customs unions, since the latter assumes a common external tariff that can divert trade from low cost suppliers outside to high cost suppliers within the union. Trade diversion in customs union theory thus becomes a negative factor for an economy and is a cost to be offset against the gains from trade creation.
[3] Zhou and Lall (2005).

Adaptability in this context implies the ability of firms to identify new market niches, to re-equip and re-train, to identify, purchase and adapt new technology and to establish alliances within international supply chains. These firm-level responses are aided by a supportive and flexible policy environment, which encourages firms to take risks, provides adequate public education, training and research expenditure, ensures firms have adequate support from the financial sector, encourages R&D activity with collaboration, where appropriate, and gives an overall strategic direction to "national competitiveness policy".

I. TRADE STRUCTURE: CHINA AND THE REGION

In general terms it is well known that China's trade and production structure is intermediate; it is less sophisticated than Japan and the first-tier of NIEs (Singapore, the Republic of Korea, and Taiwan Province of China), but in some sectors considerably more sophisticated than that of the second-tier NIEs (Indonesia, Malaysia, Thailand and the Philippines). This can be illustrated in various ways.

The simplest approach is to compare the structure of exports by trade category. Table 1 reports the correlation coefficient between shares for 3-digit SITC categories for two years 1990 (when China was still a relatively closed economy) and 2000. It can be seen that in 2000 China's export structure was relatively similar to that of Taiwan Province of China, and to a lesser extent the Republic of Korea, ten years earlier. Making the comparison for 2000 China's structure is closest to that of Taiwan Province of China and Thailand (correlation coefficients of over 0.5) and most dissimilar from that of Indonesia and the Philippines (correlation coefficients of around 0.3).

An alternative way of looking at the same data is to draw on a well-established trade classification that groups SITC categories by the technological sophistication of the products they cover based on the R&D intensity and use of natural resource of the products (for more details see Lall 2000). The significance of this means of grouping the data is that more technologically-sophisticated products (principally in the high technology category) in general tend to have higher value-added per unit of export and to show the greatest market growth in

Table 1
CORRELATION COEFFICIENTS CHINA AND REGIONAL EXPORT STRUCTURES
(3-digit SITC)

	China	
	1990	*2000*
Republic of Korea 1990	0.38	0.64
Republic of Korea 2000		0.43
Taiwan Province of China 1990	0.34	0.83
Taiwan Province of China 2000		0.53
Singapore 1990	0.10	0.42
Singapore 2000		0.41
Malaysia 1990	0.28	0.24
Malaysia 2000		0.44
Thailand 1990	0.30	0.52
Thailand 2000		0.51
Indonesia 1990	0.38	0.07
Indonesia 2000		0.33
Philippines 1990	0.23	0.38
Philippines 2000		0.33

Source: Lall and Albaladejo (2004), Table 4.

world trade; in other words the high technology category captures the most dynamic segment of world trade.

Table 2 classifies China and regional trade in 2000 by this technology grouping. Over the period 1990–2000, China's total export growth was considerably faster in the high technology category (averaging 32 per cent annually as compared with 17 per cent for all manufactures). Whilst China's growth in the high technology category (principally electronics) has been impressive, in terms of share in total manufactures it still remains well below most regional partners, with the exception of Indonesia. The importance of low technology goods in 2000 reflects the continued role of clothing and textile products based on low wage costs. This significant role is expected to continue at least in the short term with the removal of the export quota system for these goods in 2005, from which China is expected to be the main beneficiary.

Table 2
TECHNOLOGICAL STRUCTURE OF MANUFACTURED EXPORTS 2000
(In per cent)

	China	Republic of Korea	Taiwan Province of China	Singapore	Malaysia	Thailand	Indonesia	Philippines
Resource-based	9.5	11.7	4.4	14.9	13.1	18.4	33.7	6.5
Low technology	44.9	17.1	23.8	6.5	9.6	21.5	31.3	11.9
Medium technology	21.2	34.0	25.5	17.4	17.8	23.8	17.5	11.6
High technology	24.4	37.1	46.3	61.2	59.4	36.3	17.4	70.0

Source: Lall and Albaladejo (2004), Table 3 (see original for explanations of categories).

There is no simple formula for determining the degree of potential complementarity between economies, but given the differences between trade structure and the domestic production that underlie them, prima facie there seems clear scope for a re-orientation of trade in the different economies in response to the opportunities created by closer trade integration and liberalization. As we shall see, there is in fact evidence of this occurring at an accelerated pace, particularly through the segmentation of production chains in the high technology (particularly electronics) branches.

II. CHANGES IN COMPETITIVENESS IN THIRD MARKETS

China's dramatic export expansion is widely recognized and its total share of world trade has risen by 4.5 percentage points from 1990–2002 (from 1.9 to 6.4 per cent).

Like the NIEs before it, export growth has been a critical driving force for industrial development in China, since the opening of the economy to foreign trade in the early 1990s. However the role of export demand in China in the 1990s appears greater than even in the first- and second-tier NIEs at earlier stages of their development. This is illustrated by a simple demand decomposition analysis that breaks down the increase in output over a given period into growth of domestic demand, holding the import share in total supply constant, growth of exports and the import substitution effect.[4] Table 3 reports the result of this decomposition when production data are grouped by the previous technology classifications. For China the dominant role of export expansion is clear and its proportionate share generally exceeds that of the NIEs, for all but resource-based manufactured products from the second tier group who are typically net exporters of these products. A figure of 203 per cent for medium-high technology

---

[4] This is based on the identity $\Delta P = d1*\Delta S + \Delta X + (d2 - d1)*S2$, where ΔP is change in output between period 1 and 2, ΔS is change in total supply (imports plus domestic production), ΔX is change in exports, $d1$ and $d2$ are the share of domestic production in total supply in periods 1 and 2 respectively, and $S2$ is total supply in period 2. If we divide the three terms by ΔP then the ratio $(d1*\Delta S)/\Delta P$ gives the share of domestic demand in total growth, $(\Delta X/\Delta P)$ gives the share of export expansion and $((d2 - d1)*S2)/\Delta P$ gives the effect of import substitution. A negative sign on the last term means that imports are rising as a share of domestic supply and there is negative import substitution. A negative sign on the first term means falling domestic consumption.

Table 3
DEMAND DECOMPOSITION ANALYSIS OF MANUFACTURES: CHINA AND NIES
(In per cent)

Region/Time period	Category	Domestic demand	Export expansion	Import substitution
China				
1990-1994	(1)	93	18	10
	(2)	-24	164	-40
	(3)	73	48	-21
1995-1999	(1)	94	17	-11
	(2)	-30	185	-55
	(3)	4	203	-107
First-tier NIEs				
1985-1989	(1)	91	15	-6
	(2)	48	75	-23
	(3)	57	44	-2
1990-1994	(1)	103	10	13
	(2)	60	40	0
	(3)	68	34	-2
1995-1999	(1)	538	-9	-429
	(2)	85	21	-6
	(3)	58	53	-11
Second-tier NIEs				
1985-1989	(1)	99	-45	46
	(2)	66	28	7
	(3)	39	81	-20
1990-1994	(1)	77	31	-8
	(2)	59	44	-3
	(3)	48	50	2
1995-1999	(1)	61	85	-46
	(2)	12	96	-8
	(3)	22	82	-4

Source: Weiss and Jalilian (2004), Table 5.
Category: (1) Resource-based; (2) Low technology; (3) Medium and high technology.
  Note: First- and second-tier NIEs are as defined in text.

exports 1995–1999 means that the increase of exports over this period is a little more than double output expansion, because of the strong negative import substitution effect, as imports took a rising share of the domestic market for these goods in China.

This strong export growth has seen China's share of world trade rise by nearly five percentage points (1990–2002) and has undoubtedly eroded the position of many regional exporters in third-country markets, such as the United States and Japan. The most direct way of judging this competitive impact is to examine changes in market share for China and regional exporting economies. Lall and Albaladejo (2004) use a simple, but helpful, classification to organize the data. For any given market (or the world economy as a whole) five groupings are possible. The authors' terminology for this classification is as follows:

- partial threat: where China and the economy concerned gain market share, but China gains more;
- no threat: where both China and the other economy both gain market share, but with China growing more slowly;
- direct threat: where China gains market share and the other economy loses it;
- China under threat (or reverse threat) where this time China loses market share and the other economy gains;
- mutual withdrawal: where both China and the other economy lose market share.

Data on competition in the world market between China and the main NIEs is illustrated in Table 4 using these groupings. For each economy its total exports for 2000 are decomposed into these five categories.

From this data it appears that all economies have a majority of their exports (or very close to this in the case of the Philippines) under some form of "threat" as defined here. Countries in the most direct competition by this indicator are Malaysia, Thailand and Indonesia, which tend to have the least sophisticated export structures of the group. The reverse threat, where countries are gaining relative to China is modest in all cases. The countries with the more sophisticated trade structures, with a high share of high technology

Table 4
CHINA THREAT TO NIES IN THE WORLD MARKET 2000
(Percentage of total exports)

Category	Singa-pore	Taiwan Province of China	Republic of Korea	Malaysia	Thai-land	Indo-nesia	Philip-pines
Partial threat	40.4	34.0	28.0	56.5	61.6	48.3	44.0
No threat	32.0	39.3	42.2	5.0	15.9	10.7	44.3
Direct threat	23.5	22.9	26.2	28.7	15.1	19.9	5.8
Reverse threat	3.4	3.4	2.9	6.3	6.1	8.9	3.6
Mutual	0.7	0.4	0.7	3.5	1.3	12.2	2.4

Source: Lall and Albaladejo (2004), Table 6.

exports, are those where the direct threat (where the country concerned is losing market share whilst China is gaining it) is greatest, although no causal inference can be drawn from this relative change in market shares. In fact, data in the appendix to Lall and Albaladejo (2004) indicate that only in Malaysia do a majority (77 per cent) of goods under direct threat belong to the high technology category; elsewhere the majority of directly threatened goods come from low and medium technology and resource-based categories.

A more disaggregate examination of competition in third-country markets is provided by Weiss and Gao (2003). To establish the degree of loss in market share to Chinese exports, for a given country export growth for any commodity to a particular market (such as the United States or Japan) can be decomposed into a share effect (assuming the country keeps a constant share of the market) and a competitiveness effect (allowing for its changing market share). If a comparator economy (in this case China) is introduced competitiveness can, in turn, be decomposed into change in the country's market share relative to China and the change in China's market share relative to the rest of the world.[5]

---

[5] $\Delta X_{ij} = \Delta Q_i.s_{ij} + s_{ij}.Q_i^* (\Delta s_{ij}/s_{ij} - \Delta s_{ik}/s_{ik}) + \Delta s_{ik}/s_{ik}. s_{ij}.Q_i$
where X is exports and Δ is the absolute change in, Q_i is total imports of commodity i in the market concerned (at the end of the period), s_{ij} is the initial market share of country j in imports of i and with competitor country k, s_{ik} is k's market share for product i. In this expression the first term gives the share effect with market share constant, the second term gives a measure of competitiveness for country i relative to the comparator and the third term gives the competitiveness of the comparator.

This approach is applied to the exports of five ASEAN countries (Singapore, Malaysia, Thailand, Indonesia and the Philippines – henceforth the ASEAN 5) to the United States and Japan over the period 1995–2000. To illustrate the magnitude of the loss of exports to the United States due to the loss of market share relative to China, Table 5 decomposes the change in exports 1995–2000 for the five two-digit SITC categories for which, for the ASEAN 5, the absolute export loss relative to China in the United States is greatest. Change in exports in each category is set at 100, so the competitiveness effect in relation to China is a proportion of this. Columns 2 and 3 always sum to 100 as they reflect the two components of total change in exports. Competitiveness relative to China is one element of total competitiveness and when the third column has a negative sign the country is losing market share to China.

Table 5
ASEAN 5 DECOMPOSITION OF EXPORT INCREASE TO THE UNITED STATES
1995–2000

SITC	Export increase to United States	Constant market share effect	Overall competitiveness effect	Competitiveness vis-à-vis China	Export change as a percentage of 1995 exports
75	100	112	-12	-220	42
77	100	82	18	-126	55
76	100	593	-493	-572	18
89	100	574	-474	-674	10
82	100	169	-69	-197	78

Source: Weiss and Gao (2003), Table 1.
Note: SITC 75 represents office and data processing machines; 76 is telecommunications; 77 is electrical machinery; 82 is furniture; 89 is miscellaneous.

In all of these categories there has been a strong effect from the loss of market share relative to China, and in all categories except SITC 77 there is a "direct threat" in terminology used above; for SITC the threat is "partial". What is measured is the loss in exports due to the fact that a country's market share has not kept pace with that of China, as a proportion of actual export increase. In some categories the absolute value of the change in relative market share is several times the value of the actual export increase. For example, for office and data processing machines (SITC 75) the loss of exports due to the falling market share relative to China is roughly double the actual export increase achieved, whilst for telecommunications (SITC 76) it is nearly six times the actual increase. Nonetheless in all these categories, this strong loss of market share was still accompanied by rising exports from ASEAN.

The analysis of changing competitiveness relative to China can be extended by focusing on trends at the four-digit SITC level and explaining these in a regression framework linking product characteristics with changing market share relative to China. Here the dependent variable is the value of lost exports due to change in market share relative to China, scaled by division by total exports in 1995 in the same category.[6] Weiss and Gao (2003) test whether loss of competitiveness defined in this way is systematically related to the characteristics of trade categories, whether in terms of technological characteristics, or patterns of specialization. A simple model that makes competitiveness a function of the characteristics of products, as reflected in a measure of specialization, general shifts in competitiveness and changes in tastes as a demand factor, is applied. They use a measure of specialization – the relative revealed comparative advantage measure (RCA) – at the start of a period to explain changing competitiveness over the period.[7] They justify this choice because the initial RCA can be taken as a proxy for the relative output level and factor intensity of different products.

The analysis across 690 four-digit SITC categories is first conducted for the ASEAN 5 as a group and then for each economy individually. It is carried out separately for the United States and Japanese markets.

---

[6] Using the notation in footnote 3 competitiveness (COMP) is measured as:

$$COMP_{ij} = [\, s_{ij} . Q_i^* \, (\, \Delta s_{ij}/s_{ij} - \Delta s_{ik}/s_{ik}) \,] \, / \, X_{ij}$$

where X_{ij} is initial exports of i from j to the market concerned. Where there is a gain in market share relative to China, COMP will be positive and where there is a loss it will be negative.

[7] Relative revealed comparative advantage is defined as RCA = (Xij /Xtj)/(Xik/Xtk) where X refers to export value, t stands for total exports and k is the comparator economy. In principle the RCA may be related to changes in competitiveness, as defined here, either through shifts in relative factor prices or to a simple "catching up" effect. As total trade covers a wide variety of product types to impose some pattern on the data dummies are applied for nine product categories that are sub-divisions of the Lall technology classification noted above. The use of dummy variables reflecting these nine categories implies that there is broad homogeneity within each in terms of the response of different products to the explanatory variables.

The broad results strongly support the view that, not only have the main ASEAN economies been exposed to increasing competition in both the United States and Japanese markets, but also that their reduced competitiveness relative to China appear to be related systematically to particular product categories, with losses greater in the areas within those categories in which the ASEAN economies are most highly specialized relative to China.

Significantly, there is evidence of increased competition from China at both the relatively labour-intensive and the relatively high technology end of the product scale, although within a given trade category technological sophistication appears generally to offer some protection to ASEAN exporters. This latter effect is found in different products categories for different countries and appears to be most uniform for engineering products in the United States. Automobile products are the only product category for which there is no evidence of systematic loss of competitiveness because they are small in value and only a small number of observations exist. In no product category is there any evidence of systematic gains relative to China, although for a few countries and categories there is a significant cross-over rate for the RCA variable; this implies that at lower levels of specialization there is a gain of competitiveness relative to China, whilst there are losses at higher levels.

For the large categories of electronics, electrical equipment and engineering (which combined represent two-thirds of ASEAN exports in the United States and 40 per cent in Japan) there is a consistent pattern of loss of competitiveness, which is stronger in more specialized products, and which holds for all countries in both markets. In the other important categories of primary products, resource-based manufactures and textiles and garments, all countries show significant losses in either the United States or Japan and in a majority of cases for these categories countries show a significant loss in both markets. Again this is always significantly related to the degree of specialization.[8] It must be stressed that loss of competi-

---

[8] Weiss and Gao (2003) hypothesize that the link between greater specialization in ASEAN countries relative to China and loss of market share is due to shifts in the relative capital rental-wage ratios that are favourable to China and hence unfavourable to ASEAN countries. Increased domestic savings or rising FDI inflows to China, which increase the supply of capital and lower the capital rental-wage ratio, are simple candidates for a general explanation. Naturally, the industry-specific effects as well as general catch-up trends which were noted earlier may also be at work, but the analysis does not capture these.

veness as defined here refers to loss of market share relative to China. This does not necessarily convert into an absolute decline in exports. Absolute export declines for ASEAN countries are found for primary products and engineering in the United States and for primary products, resource-based manufactures, and textiles, garments and footwear in Japan. Hence much of the erosion of market share is in categories whose sales from ASEAN countries are continuing to expand, principally the very large category of electronics and electrical goods. Here losses of market share are in the product lines where ASEAN countries is most specialized, eroding established market positions.

The conclusion is that regional neighbours have been exposed to strong direct competition from Chinese exports and consequently there has been some trade diversion in the sense of relative loss of market share. Before discussing evidence on the net overall impact of closer trade integration we turn to the FDI diversion argument.

III. COMPETITION FOR FDI: IS THERE A DIVERSION EFFECT?

In recent years FDI inflows have been a major driving force in the development of East and Southeast Asian countries; some second-tier NIEs, in particular, have relied heavily on FDI for technology, management and marketing skills. The "rise of China", in terms of its attraction of heavy FDI inflows, has caused considerable concern because if there are limited FDI flows to the region, China's gains will be at the expense of its neighbours. If, as expected, foreign firms have special advantages that allow access to export markets any FDI diversion will in turn have implications for trade flows and diversion effects. Insofar as Southeast Asian economies saw declining FDI inflows in the late 1990s in the aftermath of the regional financial crisis (and net outflows in the case of Indonesia), China was the single largest developing country recipient, this concern had a superficial plausibility. However, a closer examination of the data suggests the case is greatly overstated for a number of reasons.

The absolute and relative size of FDI to China are often confused when the subject is broached. Whilst in absolute terms FDI to China is very large, once this figure is compared with either population or some measure of economic activity in the country, the ratio is not an outlier in comparison with other countries. This is seen readily in the UNCTAD FDI Performance Index, which compares a country's share in global FDI to its share in global GDP. For 1999–2000, China's figure of 1.2 is roughly the average for the region as a whole, but below the comparable figures for Singapore, Thailand and Malaysia (UNCTAD 2002, Table 2.1).

Second, this type of comparison, which is based on officially recorded FDI flows will give an upward bias to China's position since it is widely accepted that "round-tripping" – that is, the export of domestically generated funds and its return to its country of origin as FDI, is more significant in China than elsewhere. The motives for "round-tripping" in the case of China are essentially threefold: the reinvestment of flight capital that may have had its origins in the black economy; the preference to register enterprises as foreign investments to take advantage of tax incentives not available to local firms; and the wish to incorporate companies abroad (particularly in Hong Kong China) to take advantage of improved reputation, corporate governance and superior financial services. Xiao (2004) examines these issues in detail and by means of a comparison of FDI statistics in the country of origin and China, he breaks down the discrepancy into what he terms a normal "statistical error" and "round-tripping". His most likely estimate of the latter is as high as 40 per cent of FDI inflows in recent years (with high and low estimates of 50 and 30 per cent, respectively). If recorded figures are adjusted downwards by this proportion, China's FDI Performance Index figures (as defined above) will appear well below the regional average.

A simple comparison of FDI statistics and their downward adjustment as appropriate casts some doubt on the extent to which FDI to China is unusually high. However, one can address the diversion argument more rigorously by identifying the explanatory factors behind regional FDI inflows and adding a separate variable for "a China effect". Chantasasawat et al. (2003) do this by setting up a regression model which explains FDI flows to eight East and Southeast Asian economies (1985–2001) by a number of conventional variables (including measures of market size, tax rates, wage levels, human capital stock, infrastructure quality and government stability) plus FDI inflows to China.[9] If the investment diversion case is valid one will expected a significant negative coefficient on the Chinese FDI variable.

The key result of interest here is that when the level of FDI investment in the eight neighbouring economies is examined, it is positively – and not negatively – related to FDI in China. A 10 per cent increase in FDI to China raises FDI in the region by 5–6 per cent depending on specification. Rather than finding evidence of FDI diversion, it appears that FDI creation is at work. The authors explain this by referring to production networking among international firms in the region. This means that investment in China may be linked with investment elsewhere in the region to supply parts and components to plants located in China (or vice versa with China supplying parts and components to plants in one of the eight neighbouring economies). This result holds regardless of whether or not FDI from Hong Kong China, with an assumed high round-tripping element, is included in the analysis. The "China effect" is not the strongest of the factors explaining FDI inflows with measures of trade openness and taxation showing higher elasticities. Nonetheless, the significant positive sign on FDI to China is a strong undermining of the case that competition for FDI in the region is a zero-sum game. It seems preferable to view FDI flows as at least partially endogenous to regional activity, with FDI responding to the profit opportunities generated by regional growth and with FDI flows to one economy interacting positively with FDI flows to another as international firms exploit regional production sharing in a segmentation of the supply chain.

---

[9] As there will be simultaneity in the relationship with feedback between FDI to the various countries and China the model is estimated as a simultaneous equation system where:

$$AFDI_{it} = \alpha + \beta PRC\_FDI_t + \lambda x_{it} + \mu_i + e_{it} \qquad (1)$$

$$PRC\_FDI_t = \gamma + \delta AFDI_{it} + \rho z_t + v + w_t \qquad (2)$$

Here subscripts i and t refer to country i at time t; x_{it} is the set of determinants of FDI to the Asian economies covered, so for country i its FDI inflow is $AFDI_i$; z_t is the set of determinants for FDI to PRC (PRC_FDI); u_i and v are country specific terms, and e_i and w are error terms.

IV. WHAT IS THE EVIDENCE ON TRADE CREATION?

China has in recent years seen a major increase in its imports from regional neighbours and its rapid growth has been widely identified as a key source of dynamism for these countries. For example, from 1995–2003 exports of precision instruments and electrical machinery (mostly made up of parts and components) from its nine major neighbouring trade partners grew by over 600 per cent and exports of machinery, chemical products and transportation equipment grew by around 300 per cent.[10] This import growth occurred over a period of major change in trade policy in China in preparation for WTO accession. Many of the changes needed for WTO entry were introduced during the 1990s, so that the weighted average tariff on manufactures fell from 47 per cent in 1992 to 13 per cent in 2001. Under the WTO agreement this tariff is due to be reduced further to 7 per cent (expected by 2005) and the remaining non-tariff barriers are to be simplified and phased out (Martin et al. 2004).

However, establishing the link between this surge in regional imports and the trade reforms associated with WTO entry calls for more than a simple description or projection of current trade patterns. A counterfactual non-reform scenario must be compared with a projected "with reform" case. The conventional means of addressing this is to apply a form of computable general equilibrium (CGE) model that compares a baseline (pre-reform) case with scenarios based on one or more trade reform packages. Roland-Holst (2002) and (2003) applies a version of the well-known GTAP model to assess the impact of reform on trade and income for both the region and China itself.[11]

---

[10] See ADB (2004); these figures include Hong Kong China as a separate export source and are therefore slightly misleading.

[11] The model is aggregated to cover 16 countries and 18 sectors. Production sectors are based on constant returns CES production functions. Macro-growth is imposed exogenously from consensus forecasts and there are fixed government and balance of payments positions. The latter is set by exogenously given capital flows and is maintained by a change in real exchange rates which are endogenous. Productivity growth is determined partly by the imposed macro-growth rate and partly endogenously as it is assumed to be positively related to the export-output ratio by an imposed elasticity; for details see Roland-Holst (2002).

The model provides a direct comparison of "with and without scenarios" and their outcomes are driven by a combination of assumed macro-growth rates, changes in import protection (i.e. the degree of trade reform), and demand and supply patterns in the countries concerned. However, as a projection of the future it is best described as "indicative"; that is a projection of what will happen if markets clear in the way models of this type assume. As CGE models of this type assume that all markets revert to equilibrium, they imply instant adjustment as resources shift from previously protected activities, so there are no frictional underutilization problems arising from changes in trade policy. This is the perfectly competitive world in which "competitiveness" is not an issue. This is not to imply that such models give results that have no meaning, but by ignoring transitional difficulties arguably they have an implicit bias in favour of the policy they are examining.[12] Furthermore there is always the issue of whether non-tariff barriers are adequately accounted for in this type of exercise.

The major result of Roland-Holst (2002, 2003) is that in the wake of the China's WTO accession, it will have a rising trade surplus with North America and Europe up to 2020, but a rising trade deficit with ASEAN countries and with the neighbouring region more generally. Broadly speaking China will export finished goods to the former markets and import foodstuffs, raw materials, parts and components and capital goods from the latter.[13] Tables 6 and 7 illustrate the basic run of the model which compares the baseline case (i.e. projections under the assumption of no policy change) with China's WTO accession scenario.

Table 6 shows for example that China's exports to ASEAN countries are 36 per cent higher in 2020 as a result of WTO accession, while ASEAN country exports to China are 28 per cent higher. The respective percentage changes for the Republic of Korea and Taiwan Province of China (the NIEs in this context) are 43 and 32 per cent. Table 7 gives the same results now focusing on the change in the

---

[12] Modelers often respond, however, that by omitting dynamic effects relating to higher investment or capital flows these models tend to understate, not overstate, the gains from trade reform. See for example Lee et al (2004).
[13] This broad result is found in a number similar studies. See for example Ianchovichina and Martin (2003).

Table 6
TRADE GROWTH WITH CHINA WTO ACCESSION
(Percentage change from baseline scenario in 2020)

Exports to	China	Japan	NIEs	ASEAN	United States	European Union	Rest of world	Total
Exports from								
China	0	37	43	36	31	35	32	34
Japan	38	0	-4	-6	-7	-5	-5	3
NIEs	32	-10	-7	-11	-13	-10	-10	3
ASEAN	28	-4	-1	-2	-5	-3	-4	1
United States	24	-1	1	-1	0	-1	-1	1
European Union	22	0	1	-1	-2	-1	-2	0
Rest of world	13	0	2	-2	-2	-1	-1	0
Total	26	5	6	2	2	0	1	3

Source: Roland-Holst (2002), Table 4.2.
Notes: NIEs are the Republic of Korea and Taiwan Province of China.

Table 7
ABSOLUTE CHANGE IN BILATERAL TRADE BALANCE WITH CHINA IN 2020
COMPARED WITH BASELINE SCENARIO
(In 1997 US$ billions)

Country	Change in bilateral balance: China – country due to WTO accession	Projected actual bilateral trade balance China – country 2020
Japan	-4	-5
NIEs	-34	-135
ASEAN	-3	-41
United States	61	166
European Union	46	66
Rest of world	51	71

Source: Roland Holst (2002), Table 4.3 and (2003), Table 2.2.
Note: A negative sign indicates a deficit for China.

bilateral trade balance between different groupings and China as a result of WTO accession. The NIEs have a bilateral trade surplus with China in 2020 of US$34 billion as a result of WTO accession. This accounts for approximately one-third of their total projected surplus. The share of ASEAN countries explained by WTO accession is much smaller (presumably because trade barriers were lower prior to accession) at less than 10 per cent (US$3 billion out of a surplus of US$41 billion).

These results can be extended by accepting WTO accession as a given and posing the question what additional trade creation results from new regional arrangements – such as China's joining the ASEAN free trade grouping, the Asian Free Trade Area (ASEAN plus China) – or China, plus Japan and the Republic of Korea, joining ASEAN (ASEAN plus 3)? Tables 8 and 9 provide the answers in terms of percentage change in trade flows in 2020, now compared with the scenario of China's WTO accession, rather than the original baseline.

A strong growth in Chinese exports to ASEAN countries is predicted (47 per cent above the level with WTO accession alone). Import growth from ASEAN countries is only modest at 2 per cent, presumably on the basis that barriers in China are treated as already very low after WTO accession. ASEAN countries significantly reduce imports from third countries, so there is an important trade diversion effect (e.g. United States exports to ASEAN countries are 6 per cent lower and Japanese exports are 10 per cent lower). Most effects are magnified in the case of the wider group of ASEAN nations plus China, Japan and the Republic of Korea, with Chinese exports to the latter two countries rising strongly. However, the exports to China grow only modestly relative to the predicted level under WTO accession (Japan's are 2 per cent higher and ASEAN's 4 per cent). This is once more due to the fact that WTO accession is taken to have offered easy market access to exporters from these economies to China. There are now also greater diversion effects for exports of non-members than in the more limited ASEAN plus China arrangement (United States exports to ASEAN, for example fall by 9 per cent).

Table 8
TRADE GROWTH WITH CHINA JOINING ASEAN
(Percentage change from China WTO accession scenario in 2020)

Exports to	China	Japan	NIEs	ASEAN	United States	European Union	Rest of world	Total
Exports from								
China	0	-4	-4	47	-3	-4	-3	1
Japan	2	0	1	-10	1	1	1	0
NIEs	2	0	0	-12	1	1	1	0
ASEAN	2	4	3	33	3	3	1	9
United States	1	0	0	-6	0	0	0	0
European Union	1	0	0	-5	0	0	0	0
Rest of World	2	0	0	-7	0	0	0	0
Total	2	0	0	9	0	0	0	1

Source: Roland-Holst (2003), Table 3.2.

Table 9
TRADE GROWTH WITH CHINA JOINING ASEAN PLUS 3
(Percentage change from China WTO accession scenario in 2020)

Exports to	China	Japan	NIEs	ASEAN	United States	European Union	Rest of world	Total
Exports from								
China	0	21	33	27	-8	-9	-8	3
Japan	2	0	39	40	-2	-2	-2	10
NIEs	3	50	31	43	0	-1	-2	11
ASEAN	4	49	35	26	5	4	0	14
United States	5	-4	-11	-9	1	1	1	-1
European Union	4	-2	-10	-11	1	0	0	0
Rest of world	5	-9	-10	-8	1	0	1	-1
Total	4	12	10	13	-1	0	-1	2

Source: Roland-Holst (2003), Table 3.3.

Detailed information on particular sectors can also be derived from this model. If one considers the relatively inclusive regional trade grouping of ASEAN plus 3 as compared with the WTO accession scenario, Chinese exports by 2020 are higher in nine out of the 18 sectors in the model, the vast majority of total export gains are in just two sectors: processed food (US$40 billion in 1997 prices); and textiles (US$8.5 billion) (Roland-Holst 2003, Table 3.9). A disaggregated look into import and export flows at the sector level arising from the ASEAN plus 3 scenario is also possible using a simple measure "intra-industry competitiveness", essentially net exports relative to total trade in the sector.[14] Table 10 gives this measure of bilateral trade flows by sector in 2020 for the scenario of China joining ASEAN plus 3.

Table 10
INTRA-INDUSTRY COMPETITIVENESS
2020 FOR CHINA BY SECTOR AND TRADING PARTNER
(Scenario of China in ASEAN plus 3)

Sector	Japan	NIEs	ASEAN	Total
Rice	1.00	1.00	-0.94	-0.47
Other grains	1.00	1.00	1.00	-0.48
Oil seeds	1.00	1.00	1.00	-0.78
Sugar	1.00	-1.00	-1.00	-0.86
Other crops	0.96	0.92	-0.54	-0.48
Livestock	0.72	0.44	-.64	-0.51
Energy	0.96	-0.28	-0.74	-036
Processed food	0.94	0.63	-0.45	-0.15
Textiles	0.04	-0.69	0.41	-0.12
Clothing	0.89	0.73	0.99	0.92
Leather goods	0.94	-0.26	0.80	0.72
Basic manufacturing	-0.06	-0.38	0.09	-0.02
Motor vehicles	-0.81	0.52	0.76	-0.32
Other transport equipment	-0.06	-0.54	0.85	0.00
Electronic goods	-0.32	-0.42	0.02	0.06
Other manufactures	-0.11	-0.05	0.44	0.22
Construction	-0.32	0.31	1.00	-0.48
Services	0.26	0.32	0.34	0.24

Source: Roland-Holst (2003), Table 3.13.
Note: NIEs are the Republic of Korea and Taiwan Province of China.

The sectoral picture which emerges is that in general, under this scenario, China is a net importer of primary products, foodstuffs and energy and a net exporter of manufactures. This pattern is replicated in its projected trade with ASEAN countries. In the important electronics category the IIC figure 0.02 indicates a small trade surplus of 2 per cent of electronics trade (imports plus exports) between

---

[14] For sector i intra-industry competitiveness (IIC) is $IIC_i = (X_i - M_i)/X_i + M_i$, where X and M are exports and imports respectively. This figure can be given for total trade or for bilateral trade between countries x and y, so that for sector i in trade between x and y we have $IIC_{i_{xy}} = (X_i - M_i)_{xy}/(X_i + M_i)_{xy}$.

China and ASEAN countries. With respect to trade with the Republic of Korea and Taiwan Province of China there is a projected net deficit in manufactures with the important exceptions of clothing, processed food and motor vehicles. In this case there is a heavy deficit in electronics with the IIC of –0.42 indicating a trade deficit roughly 40 per cent of total trade in electronics with these two countries. Trade with Japan is projected to be in surplus with the exception of more capital and technology intensive sectors in manufacturing and construction.

Concern has been noted that closer trade links with China may push ASEAN economies down rather than up the ladder of comparative advantage into lower skill activities. Evidence from the same modeling work casts doubt on this. The IIC indicator can be adjusted to reflect differences in skilled to unskilled labour ratios between sectors, and this labour-adjusted version of the IIC can be used to classify sectors into "import dependent", "trade neutral" and "export oriented".[15] If one considers changes over the late 1990s (1996–2000) in bilateral Chinese-ASEAN country trade on the basis of skilled labour content there was a substantial shift of 16 percentage points towards greater export–orientation (which was much greater than if the unadjusted data are used). The implication is that over this period ASEAN countries were increasing their net exports to China in relatively more skill intensive activities.

Examination of trade flows alone does not indicate income or welfare changes (and may imply the "mercantilism fallacy" that exports are good and imports are bad). The modeling exercise also incorporates income change estimates calculated as future discounted income streams with a consumption and savings component. The fullest statement of these estimates can be found in Lee et al. (2004), which looks at a shorter period 2005 to 2015 and appears to use a slightly

---

[15] The adjusted figure is $ELTi_{xy} = (\lambda i^x Xi - \lambda i^y Mi)_{xy}/(\lambda i^x Xi + \lambda i^y Mi)_{xy}$ where λi^x is the skilled to unskilled labour ratio in value-added for commodity i in country x and λi^y is the same for country y. Sectors are classed as import dependent if ELTi is between –1 and –0.33, trade neutral if it is between -0.33 and 0.33, and export-oriented if it is between 0.33 and 1. See Roland-Holst and Weiss (2004).

different model specification to the earlier work.[16] Table 9 sum-
marizes the income effects by 2015 for three different scenarios:
China's unilateral removal of all remaining trade barriers (China
UNI); China joining ASEAN; and ASEAN plus 3. For 2015 the
income change by country and region for these scenarios is given
relative to the baseline (broadly the Chinese WTO accession
scenario). These estimates are given in two versions with (Table 11)
and without (Table 12) agricultural liberalization.

Table 11
INCOME EFFECTS RELATIVE TO BASELINE 2015
(Per cent change)

Country	China UNI	ASEAN plus China	ASEAN plus 3
China	2.9	1.4	4.0
Japan	0.3	0	1.6
Republic of Korea	0.6	-0.1	3.7
Taiwan Province of China	1.0	-0.3	-1.0
ASEAN	0.5	2.5	4.0
World	0.4	0.2	0.7

Source: Lee et al. (2004), Table 1.

Table 12
**INCOME EFFECTS RELATIVE TO BASELINE 2015 WITHOUT
REMOVAL OF BARRIERS ON FOOD AND AGRICULTURAL PRODUCTS**
(Per cent change)

Country	ASEAN plus China	ASEAN plus 3
China	0.9	1.9
Japan	0.1	0.7
Republic of Korea	-0.1	1.5
Taiwan Province of China	-0.3	-1.0
ASEAN	1.7	2.6
World	0.1	0.3

Source: Lee et al. (2004), Table 2.

---

[16] One difference is the inclusion of "trade costs" as a wedge between cif and fob
prices. Policy reform scenarios assume not just a removal of tariffs, but also a
lowering of trade cost, in this case by 2.5 per cent. Also in the more recent work
the baseline scenario is not very explicit and it appears to be the equivalent of
China's WTO accession in the earlier papers.

As is predictable in this type of model, since adjustment costs a assumed away, the wider the spread of the area of free trade the larger are the benefits. Hence ASEAN plus 3 is the preferred arrangement in terms of income change for all countries, apart from the excluded trading partner Taiwan Province of China. Unilateral removal of remaining tariffs by China is a superior alternative for it and the rest of the world than its entry into the limited free trade area of ASEAN, although the latter is a superior option for ASEAN countries. If agricultural trade is excluded from the reform process, benefits to all parties fall and the Republic of Korea and Taiwan Province of China can lose from China's unilateral trade liberalization.

As noted earlier these modeling exercises mask complex internal shifts in resource allocation within partner economies as trade barriers are reduced. In China this will entail potentially complex shifts within agriculture (for example in relation to grains) and in parts of manufacturing (particularly in heavy industry, parts of which are often said to be highly inefficient). These modeling exercises imply that there is ample income growth to compensate potential losers and ensure a "Pareto optimal" outcome. However, with rising inequality and a fiscally constrained state, compensation is likely to be potential rather than actual and the adjustment process will almost certainly imply winners and losers.[17] Similar points can be made concerning adjustments in partner economies.

There has been considerable concern in many countries, including China, that national domestic firms may be too small to compete in global markets. During the 1990s official policy in China identified a "national team" of 120 large enterprises to be "championed", although for a range of reasons, including restrictions on mergers and acquisitions due to intervention by provincial authorities and what was seen as forced diversification, the "national global giants" strategy has been judged a failure (Nolan 2001:187). As yet there is little evidence from the trade data that this has been a serious hindrance for the economy and that in key sectors local firms are too small to compete.

---

[17] How rapidly private sector investors emerge to take up opportunities offered by these developments on the trade front will have important implications for the actual pace and pattern of adjustment. See Kanamori and Zhao (2004) for a discussion of the evolution of the private sector in China. Kanamori (2004) discusses fiscal constraints.

...CLUSIONS

...ole evidence, as surveyed here, that China's ...n has generated substantial opportunities for trade ...estment in, regional partner economies. This rapid ...s sucked in large volumes of imports of both primary and ...iactured goods that have compensated its neighbours for their ...osses of market share in the United States and Japan. Even the concern over FDI diversion, which appeared an obvious "threat" a few years ago, can be set aside on the basis of substantial empirical evidence. Central to the growth of regional intra-industry trade has been the spread of global production networks either between units of the same firm or with independent contract manufacturers, who provide goods to the buyer's specification. Hence, final products made in China may contain parts and components from many different parts of the region with value-added at stages in a production chain that stretches across a number of countries. FDI has been a prime mover in this process in integrating Chinese-based firms in these global networks and developing the "triangular trade" between China, the rest of East and Southeast Asia and the large markets in the United States and Europe. In this emerging specialization its regional neighbours provide the inputs for manufactures from China, which are then exported out of the region. At this point in time, this is proving strongly mutually beneficial.

REFERENCES

Asian Development Bank (2004). *Outlook 2004*. New York, Oxford University Press for the Asian Development Bank (ADB).

Chantasasawat B, Fung KC, Iizaki H, Siu A (2003). International competition for foreign direct investment: the case of China. Mimeo. Santa Cruz, CA, University of California Santa Cruz. (A part of an ADB Institute Discussion Paper under preparation.)

Ianchovichina E and Martin W (2003). Economic impacts of China's accession to the WTO. *Policy Research Working Paper*, 3053. Washington DC, World Bank.

Kanamori T (2004). Fiscal reform in the People's Republic of China. *ADB Institute Research Paper*, No. 55, October. Tokyo, ADB Institute. Available at www.adbi.org.

Kanamori T and Zhao Z (2004). Private sector development in the People's Republic of China. Mimeo. Tokyo, ADB Institute, forthcoming.

Lall S (2000). The technology structure and performance of developing country manufactured exports, 1985–1998. *Oxford Development Studies*, 28(3):337–369.

Lall S and Albaldejo M (2004). China's competitive performance: a threat to East Asian manufactured exports, World Development, 32(9).

Lee H, Roland-Holst D and van der Mensbrugghe D (2004). The implications of prospective free trade agreements in East Asia. Mimeo.

Martin W, Bhattasali D and Li S (2004). China's accession to the WTO: impacts on China. In Krumm K and Kharas H, eds., *East Asia Integrates: A Trade Policy Agenda for Shared Growth*. New York, Oxford University Press for the World Bank.

Nolan P (2001). *China and the Global Economy*. London, Palgrave.

Roland-Holst D (2002). An overview of PRC's emergence and East Asian trade patterns to 2020. *ADB Institute Research Paper*, No. 44, October. Tokyo, ADB Institute. Available at www.adbi.org.

Roland-Holst D (2003). East Asian trade relations in the wake of China's WTO accession. Mimeo. Tokyo, ADB Institute.

Roland-Holst D and Weiss J (2004). ASEAN and China: export rivals or partners in regional growth? *World Economy*, 27(8):1255–1274, August.

UNCTAD (2002). *World Investment Report 2002: Transnational Corporations and Export Competitiveness*. United Nations publication, Sales No. E.02.II.D.4, New York and Geneva.

Weiss J and Gao Shanwen (2003). China's export threat to ASEAN. *ADB Institute Discussion Paper*, No 2, October. Tokyo. Available at www.adbi.org.

Weiss J and Jalilian H (2004). Industrialization in an age of globalization: some comparisons between East and South East Asia and Latin America. *Oxford Development Studies*, 32(2). First presented at the LAEBA Conference at ADB Institute, September 2003. Available at www.adbi.org.

Xiao Geng (2004). Roundtripping foreign direct investment in the People's Republic of China. *ADB Institute Discussion Paper*, No. 7. Tokyo, Available at www.adbi.org.

Zhou Yuping and Lall S (2005). The impact of China's FDI surge on FDI in South-East Asia: Panel data analysis for 1986–2001. *Transnational Corporations*, 14(1), UNCTAD/ITE/IIT/2005/1, April. United Nations publication, New York and Geneva.

WHY IS CHINA THE WORLD'S NUMBER ONE ANTI-DUMPING TARGET?

Yuefen Li[1]

Abstract

This paper examines how the inherent weakness and loopholes of anti-dumping laws have allowed multinational enterprises to use it as a weapon to squeeze out new market entrants and strengthen monopoly. Though the benefits of China's trade expansion have been distributed much more broadly than some early industrializers, China has been a number one target of anti-dumping activities in the world. Being a new and relatively efficient new rivalry in the world market may be an important reason. On the other hand, China's development stage and its trade structure also place it at a disadvantage when it comes to anti-dumping activities.

INTRODUCTION

The first anti-dumping investigation against China was launched by the European Community in 1979, immediately after China started opening its economy to the outside world. Since then, the filing of contingent protection measures targeted at China have proliferated at a rapid pace, with anti-dumping actions far more prevalent than other measures such as safeguards. In the 1980s, anti-dumping cases against China averaged 6.3 per year. The number increased to 30.3 per year in the 1990s.[2] From 1996 up to the present day, China has ranked first in the world in anti-dumping investigations and final measures against its exports. In 2004, there were 48 anti-dumping investigations and 41 final measures against exports from China,[3] once again at the top of the list. It is worth noting, however, that in 2004 the gap between China's position at the head of the list and the country in the number two slot, the Republic of Korea, was huge: With its 12 anti-dumping measures against its exports, the Republic of Korea held a distant second place to China's 48 anti-dumping investigations.

---

[1] The author is grateful to Alicia Rapin-Orrego for statistical assistance, Victor Ognivtsev for comments and suggestions. The opinions expressed in this paper are those of the author and do not necessarily reflect the views of UNCTAD. The author remains solely responsible for any shortcomings in this paper.

[2] China is facing non tariff barrier, accessed on 16 July 2003. For details see www.cei.gov.cn.

[3] WTO press releases No. 387, 1 November 2004 and No. 406, 19 May 2005.

The cost of anti-dumping activities against Chinese exports is high. From 1979 up to October 2002, 33 countries initiated 544 anti-dumping and safeguard cases and measures against Chinese exports affecting more than 4,000 products with a value of around US$16 billion.[4] However, this amounted to only about 5 per cent of China's total exports, and was not extensive enough to cripple the economy.

An analysis follows on the major factors contributing to China's position as number one target of anti-dumping investigations in the world over the past consecutive few years.

I. EXTERNAL FACTORS

I.1.   Anti-dumping laws could be used to benefit multinational enterprises and victimize late industrializers

As laws are not amended as frequently as developments take place, it is not uncommon for them to be manipulated and abused by contemporaries. However, when laws are too outdated, they may give rise to incidences of running counter to the very principles on which the law was introduced.

Many countries have amended their anti-dumping (AD) laws in recent years. The WTO Agreement on Anti-dumping was endorsed in 1994, only a relatively short time ago. However, some of the basic economic assumptions of international trade conducted in the 18th century are still the cornerstone of the AD laws. That is what a recent McKinsey study[5] describes as a "residency-based view of trade", which means that exports are goods and services leaving a nation's borders, regardless of nationality and ownership of producers and service-providers involved, while imports are the mirror of exports. However, these basic assumptions no longer apply to a large part of international trade because of the tremendous changes that have occurred since the days of barter trade and the time when the first anti-dumping laws were introduced. Multinational enterprises (MNEs) have increasingly begun to offshore their production

---

[4] *People's Daily*, 24 June 2003: Frequent anti-dumping bangs, perfecting early warning system is a must.
[5] Farrell et al. (2005)

activities and trade between affiliates and their parent companies have mushroomed.

A significant portion of the goods and services exported from a country do not really belong to that particular country. With FDI, companies no longer need to cross national borders to sell their products. A volume of cross-border trade directly associated with the determination of dumping action no longer accurately reflects actual commercial activities between two trading nations. Not to take these changes and factors into consideration in AD laws may result in the unwelcoming outcome of not meeting the intended purpose of legislators when they enacted the law. Anti-dumping duties were conceived in Canada at the beginning of the 19th century with the intention of maintaining a "level playing field" for domestic industries whose activities essentially took place within national frontiers. Subsequently, they were extended to cover transactions from outside the national borders. However, as pointed out by Richard J. Pierce Jr, globalization and the rise of MNEs has meant that in many cases anti-dumping laws have been administered and manipulated to "facilitate the formation, maintenance, and enforce-ment of cartels."[6]

One common feature of anti-dumping laws/agreements is that they have sufficient loopholes to allow MNEs to use them to squeeze out efficient new market rivals. This is one important reason why major newly-industrializing economies (NIEs) experienced a time when they were the targets of contingent protection measures; this came at a time when they underwent fast economic growth and foreign trade expansion, which quite often forced them to set up foreign direct investment (FDI) operations abroad. China has entered such a period, but has not yet developed the capacity to engage in large scale FDI to avoid anti-dumping activities.

The internationalization and segmentation of production chains and the rise of MNEs have rendered anti-dumping laws antiquated. On the whole, anti-dumping laws/agreements have placed countries that have few MNEs and countries that are new entrants to the global market at a very disadvantageous position. MNEs are demanders of export prices and also have the capability to collude against a particular product from a developing country. These enterprises do so by using

---

[6] Pierce (1999:2).

contingent protection measures, thereby creating instability and uncertainty for developing countries' exports such as reductions in trade volumes, losing market shares for their goods and, in some cases the countries' totally withdrawing from the market. MNEs have used anti-dumping measures as an instrument to strengthen their monopoly.[7]

The costs of anti-dumping measures on the domestic economies of the targeted countries in terms of financial losses and human suffering when workers are laid off are much larger for developing countries than for industrial countries. For the initiating countries, the protection it affords its domestic producers is limited. It is true that a number of developing countries, including China, have also become major initiators of anti-dumping investigations; however, more often than not, this was because domestic industries find it hard to adjust to a highly competitive environment. Without large MNEs, they are not in a position to use anti-dumping to create a monopoly in a certain market.

I.2.   MNEs can jump tariffs and avert anti-dumping via their foreign affiliates

Dramatic changes have taken place in the global economy since the promulgation of the first anti-dumping law in Canada. The rise of MNEs and progress made in technology and communication has fundamentally changed the landscape of global production supply chains. Production is now globalized and segmented. Component and service inputs and assembly operations involved in the production of a traded product can now take place in different countries. The growing integration of national economies, a process known as globalization, is mainly coordinated by MNEs through FDI and, to a lesser extent, by other contractual arrangements. An important part of FDI is market oriented which means that affiliates of MNEs sell products directly to host-country markets, thus jumping both tariff and non-tariff barriers including anti-dumping concerns. This renders outdated the concept of trade balance since it does not cover the goods and services sold by MNEs in FDI host countries, even though these can be very significant.

---

[7] Messerlin (2002).

MNE affiliates in host countries are treated as residencies of these countries. Their local sales, regardless of whether they are goods or services, are not considered as exports and are therefore not included in the trade balance. In cases when these affiliates export goods and services produced in the FDI host countries to their home countries, they would be reflected in the trade balance as exports of the FDI host country to the MNE affiliates' home country. According to an article published by McCaughrin (2004) (Figure 1):

> Nearly three times as many goods are sold overseas by US foreign affiliates as by US exporters. Incorporating foreign affiliate sales reduces the US deficit by almost a full percentage point of GDP. US multinationals are not alone in relying on affiliates to distribute goods overseas. Japanese multinationals exported \$325bn of goods during the first three quarters of 2003. But on top of that, Japanese affiliates sold an additional \$287bn of goods (excluding sales back to Japan) that are not captured in the trade balance.[8]

Figure 1
SALES OF SERVICES AND GOODS OF UNITED STATES AFFILIATES IN CHINA 1989–2001

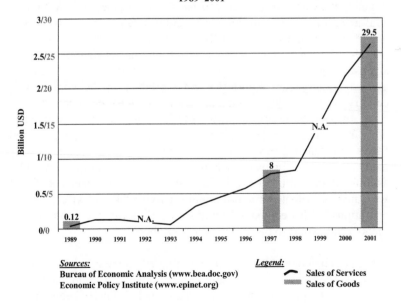

Sources:
Bureau of Economic Analysis (www.bea.doc.gov)
Economic Policy Institute (www.epinet.org)

Legend:
⌒ Sales of Services
▬ Sales of Goods

---

[8] McCaughrin (2004).

So for the MNEs, in addition to the various incentives offered by the host countries, the goods and services sold directly in foreign markets by their affiliates are not included in the bilateral trade balance, thus minimizing domestic political pressure on host countries to take contingent protection against them. This makes for a major criteria to impose contingent protection such as "material injury" to domestic producers, "import surge" and "market disruption" less relevant. Japanese FDI flows to the European Union and the United States in the 1980s were positively affected by the overall increase in the number of anti-dumping actions in the two jurisdictions. This may explain why Japan's position in the anti-dumping investigations league tables fell from its number one position for the period of 1981–1997 to the fourth position for the period of 1995–2001.[9] In addition, once production facilities have been set up in these jurisdictions, they can file anti-dumping petitions under local anti-dumping laws against foreign rivals. China, being a developing country, still relies heavily on exports to promote its economic development.

As MNEs have production facilities located in different parts of the world, they are also capable of dodging anti-dumping activities targeted at exports from their affiliates. For instance, if a MNE has had an affirmative anti-dumping ruling against products it has manufactured in China, the MNE could redirect the product to a market other than the one with anti-dumping restrictions in place against the product made in China. Meanwhile, its affiliate located in a third country can export the same product to the complaining country with a product originating from a country other than China. Thus, through trade diversion, the MNE could survive positive anti-dumping rulings without losing market share. In 2003, the United States threatened to levy dumping charges on some colour TV sets made in China, a company such as Philips exported large screen TVs assembled in China to the United States, its Chairman and Chief Executive said that the anti-dumping activity "do not affect Philips operations" as his company "could shift TV production to its Mexico plants" and export to the US market from there.

It needs to be pointed out that foreign funded companies in China can normally be spared anti-dumping litigations or be obliged to pay much lower anti-dumping duties than their Chinese counterparts,

---

[9] Zanardi (2004).

as they can prove that they are operating in a market economy environment.

I.2.a) MNEs use "domestic industries" to initiate anti-dumping investigations

Another phenomenon which goes hand in hand with globalization and growing interdependence is that, so-called "domestic industries" are, in many cases, no longer purely domestic. They very often have similar and varied ties with MNEs, e.g. shareholding and contractual assembling operations. They can even sometimes be affiliates of MNEs based in a complaining country. Vested interests give rise to suspicions of collusion to snatch market share from competitors. One example is the anti-dumping investigation against Chinese colour TVs in the United States. As pointed out by the head of the International Brotherhood of Electrical Workers, the trade union supporting the anti-dumping filing, "the majority of TV manufacturing in the U.S. is multinational. There are very few American companies producing TVs."[10] Labour unions at Sanyo Manufacturing in Arkansas, Sharp Electronics in Tennessee and Toshiba America in New Jersey are all Japanese firms that have a part to play in the case against Chinese TV producers. Because of this, there has been "a widespread suspicion among the China industry that Japanese companies were behind the case."[11] Thus the "domestic industry" is most probably the extension of Japanese multinationals which have invested in the United States market to jump tariffs and anti-dumping measures and are being threatened by the Chinese imports. The possibility exists that Japanese multinationals were using anti-dumping as a weapon to protect their market share in the United States.

I.2.b) MNEs collude in anti-dumping activities to squeeze out new market entrants

MNEs, through their affiliates, often collude with each other to squeeze out new foreign market entrants, particularly new and weak entrants from developing countries. In 1998 Maur wrote that ...

---

[10] See IBEW website: http://www.ibew.org/stories/03journal/030708/p12b.htm.

[11] *China Daily*, 20 April 2004: Final ruling fails to surprise. By Dai Yan.

> ... collusion between firms operating in several countries and deciding to hit jointly a common foreign rival-especially when these firms do not occupy a dominant position in their respective markets could be another hypothesis for explaining multiple overseas petitions. We can imagine that MNE firms meeting in a specific market may agree to coordinate their strategies against a common rival. Some instances of "echoing" could support that hypothesis. [12]

This explains why most NIEs are targets of anti-dumping activities or have experienced a period of intense trade friction with major industrialized countries. China is also going through a period of heavy reliance on foreign trade to promote economic growth and industrialization. The table on ratio of share of anti-dumping investigations and share of export value shows that China's ratio of share of anti-dumping investigations is very high in relation to its share of world trade. This could support the hypothesis that it is a target of anti-dumping and that China is, in fact, faring worse than NIEs. According to its WTO accession agreement, China will continue to be treated as a non-market economy until 2016. China's non-market economy status makes it an even easier target of MNE collusion, as "surrogate values" for anti-dumping ruling are always obtained from a third party in "comparable market-economy countries". MNEs sometimes succeeded in getting companies related to the enterprises in the complaining country to provide surrogate values. Several studies documented cases of collusion against Chinese exports (Maur, 1998). One extreme example of this is the potassium permanganate case when Asturquimica, the sole European producer, filed a complaint in March 1986 against Chinese imports of this product. Asturquimica had been itself previously hit by a duty in a similar procedure in the United States. Asturquimica then asked for the cooperation of Carus Chemicals Co. in order to establish third market value determination in the investigation. Carus Chemicals, precisely the sole United States producer and the firm that petitioned against Asturquimica a few years back, agreed to cooperate. The respondents opposed, in vain, the choice of Carus as surrogate firm.[13] This is an example of how European enterprises colluded with the United States against Chinese producers.

---

[12] Maur (1998), p. 17.
[13] Maur (1998), p.18.

RATIO OF SHARE OF ANTI-DUMPING INVESTIGATIONS AND SHARE OF EXPORT VALUE

Country	Share of anti-dumping investigations in total world investigations (Per cent)				Export share of total world exports (Per cent)				Ratio of share of anti-dumping investigations and the share of export value			
	1981-1987	1988-1998	1998-2002	1981-2002	1891-1987	1988-1998	1998-2002	1981-2002	1891-1987	1988-1998	1998-2002	1981-2002
China	4.15	10.97	13.59	9.40	1.45	2.36	4.00	2.44	2.86	4.65	3.40	3.85
Japan	8.88	5.88	4.42	6.50	6.92	8.68	6.98	7.74	1.28	0.68	0.63	0.84
Republic of Korea	5.16	6.89	7.96	6.58	1.46	2.17	2.51	2.03	3.53	3.18	3.17	3.24
Taiwan Province of China	4.06	4.60	5.25	4.58	1.20	2.15	2.14	1.84	3.38	2.14	2.45	2.49
United States	8.71	8.53	4.36	7.64	14.63	11.76	11.90	12.70	0.60	0.73	0.37	0.60

Sources: UN Comtrade Database, WTO Anti-dumping Gateway (www.wto.org), Zanardi (2002) and UNCTAD calculations.

MNEs are also capable of creating a dumping scenario to take advantage of a protected market after a positive ruling of dumping. There were cases when foreign firms chose to increase the likelihood that trade barriers would be erected against its own industry, as this could be an optimal strategy if the firm could then shift production to the protected country and tariff jump thereby giving them the edge over competing foreign firms unable to engage in FDI. The mechanism is a simple one. When MNEs spot a new efficient entrant to the market, they purposely reduce their sales in that market in order to fabricate a proof of injury in the investigation stage of an anti-dumping petition. Then, after anti-dumping restrictive measure forced the new rival to withdraw from the market, they would re-enter the much more protected market. This is a strategic way for MNEs to maximize their profit margin and optimize their monopoly.

I.2.c) Pressure by MNEs on developing downstream producers could lead to dumping charges

Globalization has hastened the growth of buyer-driven commodity chains that connect advanced country marketing or retail companies with contractors manufacturing in low-cost developing economies.[14] Very often the lead firm is a brand name merchandiser or a large retailer in a developed country which orchestrates the procurement, manufacture and marketing of products manufactured by contractors, and sub-contractors in developing countries. Because of China's cost advantages, in particular low labour cost, China has become an important downstream producer in these global commodity chains. However, one of the constant pressures facing those at the lower end of the commodity chain is the incessant demands by brand name merchandisers and large retail distributors for lower export prices. If these demands are not met the producers risk losing the contracts; and Chinese firms have little bargaining power as they depend on the demands of MNEs. As noted by Gereffi, the powerful influence of the lead firm in shaping contractor relations is indisputable.[15] A recent article by Harney, an excerpt of which is found below, clearly illustrates this unequal relationship:

---

[14] Frenkel (2001)
[15] Gereffi et al. (1999).

> The pressure on Chinese factories, already the lowest-cost factories in the world, to supply goods even more cheaply is enormous. Chan Ka Wai, Associate Director of the Hong Kong Christian Industrial Committee, a working conditions lobbying group, estimates the prices international toy companies and retailers demand when ordering from China have fallen by 30 per cent over the past three years. "... Five years ago, a reasonable profit would have been a gross margin of about 25 per cent" says Mr. Leung, who pays his 7,000 workers an average of RMB 500–600 a month. "Nowadays, all I can get is 5–10 per cent. ..." He adds "We want to work with [the multinationals] because they order such big quantities. But if they keep squeezing us, it may not work.[16]

By pressuring Chinese suppliers, these retailers and wholesalers may very well widen their profit margins. However, they also push Chinese suppliers into a very unpleasant anti-dumping petition. All the same, when it comes to anti-dumping investigations, the tendency would be to blame Chinese enterprises for taking away jobs of the complaining countries instead of wholesalers or retailers of the complaining country trying to optimize their bottom lines.

I.2.d) Developing exporters are negatively affected by fight between foreign interest groups

In a number of anti-dumping cases against Chinese enterprises, those enterprises involved were caught between the conflicts of the various domestic interests of the complaining country. Two recent anti-dumping cases inspired by the United States against Chinese wooden bedroom furniture and colour TV illustrate this. In the case for furniture, the United States Department of Commerce noted that the anti-dumping petition on Chinese wooden bedroom furniture has split the furniture manufacturing and retail industries as companies are taking sides in the political battle. The United States Furniture Retailer Association published an article on its website which reveals that the manufacturers, including some petitioners, were responsible for establishing the Chinese furniture export industry years ago by sharing designs and exporting production facilities.

---

[16] Harney (2004).

They negotiated the lowest possible prices from the Chinese and resold the imported furniture, supplementing their own production lines, to large and small American retailers at a 30 to 40 percent profit. These middleman profits were in addition to the profits they earned by selling the furniture within their own product lines. ... Over the past several years, the Chinese have established direct channels with retailers and other customers in the US. As the petitioners lost their position as middleman they are now attempting to reclaim this role by shutting off Chinese imports by filing the dumping case.[17]

When the United States International Trade Commission announced a positive ruling in January 2004, the same article on the website of the United States Furniture Retailer Association added that

Contrary to the domestic producers' claims of protecting and returning jobs to the U.S., these same domestic producers are already setting up importing programs in other countries such as Brazil, Chile, Vietnam and Indonesia. These actions undermine the claims of returning jobs to the US.

The furniture case proves that trade protection, in many cases, should be seen more as a conflict between domestic forces (namely export interests versus import-competing interests) than a conflict between countries.[18] From the initial rulings it seems that manufacturers had greater political influence than retailers. This is most probably because retailers are more fragmented and not as united as manufacturers.

I.2.e) Anti-dumping activities redistribute trade instead of protecting domestic industries

The rise of MNEs and four decades of trade liberalization also render anti-dumping ineffective in protecting domestic industries. Indeed, anti-dumping measures can cost exporters dearly and can even totally exclude them from a market as shown by the EuropeanUnion anti-dumping rulings against Chinese color TVs and bicycles. Because of this, anti-dumping has risen in prominence as an instrument for imposing import restrictions. However, trade diversion from other producers can fill the vacuum within a very short period of time.

---

[17] Historical background: Chinese bedroom furniture imports and the United States furniture industry. See for more detail www.furnitureretailers.org.
[18] Messerlin (2002), p. 7.

Modern technology and communication, and segmentation of the production chain can all in one way or another facilitate the process. So what "the injured domestic producers" get from a positive ruling is mostly just a breathing space of very limited duration. On top of this, due to increasing interdependence, anti-dumping actions also have had a negative impact on other interest groups of the complaining country.

As demonstrated in the United States furniture case against China, wholesalers, retailers and wood exporters in the United States suffer at the same time as Chinese furniture manufacturers. The only beneficiaries are the United States furniture manufacturers. For exports with high import contents, the characteristic of Chinese exports, all of the parties involved in the production chain will, to some extent, be negatively affected by anti-dumping rulings. And as shown by the furniture case, more often than not, the type of trade restrictions seen today end up redistributing trade, disproportionately penalizing one country while rewarding another, without necessarily achieving the original objective of protecting the industry intended.

I.3.   Trade liberalization, contingent protection and newly industrializing economies

China's impressive expansion of international trade started in the late 1970s, when two decades of trade liberalization had already resulted in considerably lower tariff levels in many countries. Since then further deepening of trade liberalization has reduced significantly the importance of tariff as a trade barrier. As anti-dumping activities can be invoked relatively easily and selectively compared to other trade measures, and as anti-dumping investigations, regardless of the nature of their final rulings, can lead to almost immediate loss of market share on the part of exporting countries, they have also become the most frequently used trade remedies. By the 1990s anti-dumping had become a major instrument of trade protection for developed countries. Since the WTO Agreements went into effect in 1995, this instrument has become increasingly popular in all countries. So while trade liberalization opens doors for late industrializers, anti-dumping, safeguard, and countervailing measures could also be used to deter or harass late industrializers, and China included.

Both developed and developing country governments have been encouraging and supporting domestic producers to use anti-dumping as a mechanism to protect their markets. Developing countries started to enact anti-dumping laws and tried to raise awareness on anti-dumping practices. Developed countries have made anti-dumping activities more user-friendly. Some have even provided incentives to the users of anti-dumping measures. In the United States, amendments to anti-dumping law have made it easier for domestic firms to prove the existence of dumping, including extensions of the definition of "less than fair value" to include both international price discrimination and sales below cost.[19] Moreover, the United States has a legislation, the Byrd Amendment, designed to give anti-dumping duties collected by the United States Customs Service to private companies that filed anti-dumping petitions. In the fiscal year 2003, United States Customs and Border Protection paid out US$190 million in Byrd Amendment claims.[20] It is a *de facto* subsidy to anti-dumping petitioners, as indicated in the WTO ruling in April 2004.

Given this kind of international environment at a time when China was going through fast trade expansion, it is not surprising that it has become the world's number one target for anti-dumping activities. However, as we will see in the next section, China's specific trade and economic structure has also contributed to the skyrocketing anti-dumping charges against its exports.

II. DOMESTIC FACTORS CONTRIBUTING TO THE UTILIZATION OF CONTINGENT PROTECTION MEASURES AGAINST CHINESE EXPORTS

II.1. Fast trade growth of standard basic goods with heavy market concentration

From 1978 to 2002, China's exports increased around 12 per cent on a year-on-year basis – much higher than the world average (Figure 2). Even so the parallels between China, Japan and the Republic of Korea are overdrawn, as trade expansion by Japan and Korea grew at an even higher rate during their peak periods. China's trade expansion is …

---

[19] Prusa and Skeath (2002:4).
[20] See www.cbp.gov/xp/cgov/import/add_cvd/cont_dump/cdsoa_03/ of the United States Customs and Border Protection agency.

... not unprecedented in either its scope or speed. In fact, by some indicators, China's experience is less dramatic than that of Japan and Korea during their period of industrialization and integration with the global economy.[21]

Figure 2
TRADE EXPANSION IN CHINA FROM 1982–2004

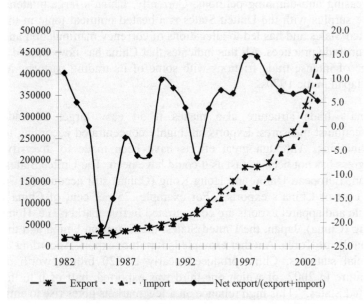

— ✳ — Export · · ▲ · · Import ——◆—— Net export/(export+import)

Source: IMF DOT, February 2005.
Note: Estimates for 2004 are based on the 9-month cumulative value of 2004 over the same period in 2003 Note on World Exports in EIU: "... in November 2004 (year-to-year) exports grew by 46 per cent."

Moreover, as China is positioned at the lower end of the international supply chain, producing predominantly labour-intensive goods and, as foreign-funded enterprises[22] account for around half of its imports and exports, the benefits of its trading with the rest of the world is more spread than those of Japan and the Republic of Korea which have a greater proportion of high-tech exports and have control of

---

[21] Rumbaugh and Blancherm (2004:5).
[22] Foreign funded enterprises include equity joint ventures, wholly foreign-owned enterprises and joint exploration companies for special extraction industries. They range from large transnational corporations to small and medium-sized enterprises owned mainly by investors of Chinese ethnic origin from East Asia.

almost the entire supply chain for some products. Unlike these two countries, China had welcomed FDI; Chinese exports have high import contents; and the country's current account has been largely in balance, though a surplus on current account overall has been increasing in recent years. However, while it is not an unprecedented, China's sharp increase of trade within a relatively short period of time is still quite remarkable. Not surprisingly, this event has given rise to increasing anti-dumping petitions. Currently, China's large bilateral trade surplus with the United States is a heated political topic in the United States and has led to allegations of currency manipulation and unfair trade practices. All this indicates that China has now entered a stage of intense trade frictions with some of its trading partners, as did Japan in the 1970s.

China's trade structure also makes it an easy target of trade protectionist measures. Exports are highly concentrated according to destinations. Although great efforts have been made to diversify, progress has not been as fast as it could have been. The United States, Japan, European Union and Hong Kong (China) still account for 70 per cent of China's exports.[23] For example, 75 per cent of China's textile and apparel exports are concentrated in five markets, i.e. Hong Kong (China), Japan, the United States, the European Union and the Republic of Korea. Another example is furniture export. According to official statistics, China produced nearly US$20 billion worth of furniture in 2002, of which one-third was exported, half of it to the United States.[24] This high reliance on a few markets gives rise to anti-dumping pressure (Figure 3).

As for export product categories, up to the first half of 1990s China's exports had the characteristics of an economy undergoing the initial stages of industrial development. There were almost no brand products and little high value added. Exports were mostly labour intensive and composed of standard and basic products. However, these were also the products of sunset industries in industrialized countries that have become the object of intensive/vigorous anti-dumping claims. Anti-dumping investigations can win time and allow market share for those industries in developed countries to adjust as this normally will take longer with protection. United States anti-

---

[23] See for more details *China Economic Information Network* at www.cei.gov.cn.
[24] *China Daily* (Hong Kong edition), 6 November 2003: Furniture makers to fight dumping charges.

Figure 3
EXPORT DESTINATIONS

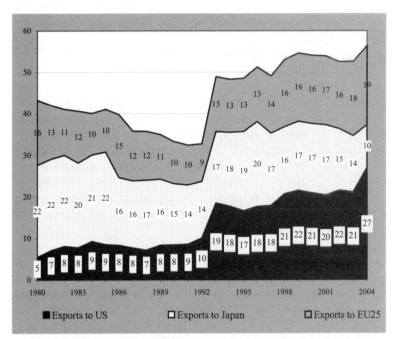

Source: IMF DOT February 2005.
Note: Estimates for 2004: based on the 9-month cummulative value of 2004 over same period in 2003 Note on WORLD exports in EIU: "...in November 2004 (year-to-year) exports grew by 46 per cent."

dumping investigations against Chinese steel went on for a whole year and even though the final verdict was in China's favour, the damage was done. Some customers were lost and the stocks of the Chinese enterprises involved went into free fall on the stock market.

According to a Chinese Government source, 70 to 80 per cent of the total anti-dumping investigations against China are concentrated on textiles, chemicals, steel and mineral sectors, all of which are labour intensive and low value added sectors of productivity. Most of these are the sunset industries in developed countries that are at the same time the mainstay industries for countries undergoing the first stages of industrialization. In the past three years, chemicals and metals still ranked foremost for anti-dumping investigations. Messerlin found that anti-dumping measures in metals, chemicals, machinery and electrical equipment, textiles and clothing, and plastics accounted for

75 per cent of the total number of measures.[25] He also noticed that these products are characterized by a high proportion of relatively standard production and oligopolistic structures. He suspects that complaining firms use anti-dumping as an instrument to segment the market and squeeze out new rivals.

II.2. The diminishing role of the State

Ironically, although China has been treated as a non-market economy by some of its trading partners, the diminishing role of Government in production planning and the foreign trade has also led to duplicate investments and overcapacity. The Government is no longer directly involved in foreign trade although it continues to monitor its operations at an arms' length. For most export products, the Government's present function is to maintain a registry system. Manufacturers' associations have not acquired the capacity to influence production activities.

An increasing number of Chinese firms in the export sector are operating in a market environment where the purchase of inputs and the raising of finance are founded on commercial principles. Exporting enterprises however have yet to learn to operate more systematically – i.e. by conducting feasibility studies and business planning. Herd behaviour is prevalent; once a producer enters a major market, many others follow. In the process, not much attention has been paid to the overall volume and value increase in the export market. For example, according to United States manufacturers bedroom furniture exports into the country tripled to US$1.4 billion between 2000 to 2003.[26] Further, the United States International Trade Administration data indicate that the export of colour TV into the country had increased from 56,295 units in 2001 to 1,759,684 in 2003 – an increase of over 31 times within a period of three years.[27] These huge increases do easily trigger anti-dumping petitions. Thus there is still a lot to learn for the Government to perfect its use of fiscal, financial, legal and administrative measures that are allowed by WTO rules in order to guide the economy to maintain a rational

---

[25] Messerlin (2002).
[26] *Business Week*, 21 June 2004: Wielding a heavy weapon against China.
[27] Fact Sheet, United States International Trade Administration, Department of Commerce, Anti-dumping Duty orders to be issued on the anti-dumping duty investigation on certain colour television receivers from the People's Republic of China. In: www.ita.doc.gov, accessed July 22 2004.

and balanced increased rate of fixed asset investments and so secure a stable and sustained development of the foreign trade sector.

Many exporting companies lack a good understanding of WTO Rules of Origin. As a result, the "Made in China" label was placed on exports which were, in fact, not really up to the threshold set by the Rules of Origin. This consequently has artificially boosted the actual volume of Chinese exports. With this working environment, the education of exporters and the enforcement of such rules should in principle form part of the Government's responsibilities.

In addition, the majority of enterprises resort to price competition for market entry and market expansion in both domestic and international markets. Price wars in the Chinese market are sometimes even more intense than abroad and grow beyond the normal bounds of competition which degenerate into a chaotic suicidal turf war among enterprises. Colour television was one of the most notable casualties of price wars, making the Chinese colour television industry one of the most market-oriented in China. Product upgrading and differentiation is yet to be utilized as a tool to capture and maintain market share. A significant part of Chinese exports is still con-centrated in such anti-dumping intensive products as textiles, clothing, footwear and travel items. One important reason for this phenomenon is that most of these products have low market entry cost. As product upgrading requires research and development and the recovery of this kind of sunk cost will take time, companies tend to avoid this type of strategic investment. Instead, there is a tendency for domestic entrepreneurs to rush to produce the same products at about the same time, thereafter creating a highly competitive situation. More often than not, exports are priced at extremely low levels with razor thin profits. Some anti-dumping charges may have been well substantiated because intense price competition in China may push enterprises into periods of selling at a loss.

Due to reasons such as lack of funds and the lack of highly skilled human resources, export enterprises still rely on one of the most important absolute advantage they possess when engaging in price competition – low labour cost. Price wars very often end up with raw material suppliers and workers bearing the brunt of cost cutting. For example, in 2003 some 98 million migrant peasants had left their hometowns to seek jobs in urban areas. This movement has presently given China an absolute advantage in terms of cheap labour.

However, keeping wage level very low is not only unethical but such a low level of income also has a negative impact on domestic consumption level. Here again it is the responsibility of Government to enforce minimum employment standards.

II.3. Processing trade is prone to trade frictions

The growing importance of processing trade

China's heavy concentration of exports destinations as well as its dramatic expansion of trade are closely related with the rising importance of processing trade.

Unlike Japan and the Republic of Korea which emphasized the development of their national brands and their own national giants with horizontal and vertical production specialization, i.e. with the entire production process undertaken within their countries, China's trade expansion has relied heavily on processing trade. Although efforts have been made to transform large SOEs into "pillar industries" and then into globally competitive giants, the fact remains that by 2004, China only had 14 companies on the list of Fortune 500 top global firms, all of them SOEs and mainly active in the heavy industry and telecommunication sectors.[28] Not only do Japanese companies on the same list dwarf these 14 Chinese SOEs, they also fall significantly behind global leaders in sales revenue, profits and R&D (Nolan 2002). As mentioned in a major survey carried out in 2004 by the British Engineering Employers' Federation (EEF), a major manufacturers' association in the United Kingdom:

> In contrast to the challenges from developed countries, it is likely that UK companies are facing competition from Chinese-based rather than Chinese-owned companies. To date there are few global Chinese companies of note providing UK-based manufacturers with a significant degree of competition. Companies that reported China as a current threat to their business saw this coming through customer demands for lower prices to a much greater degree than competition in the export or domestic markets.[29]

---

[28] *Oxford Analytica*, 15 March 2005: China: SOE reforms to create national champions.

[29] EEF (Engineering Employers' Federation, a manufacturer's organization in the United Kingdom. Where Now for Manufacturing? A survey which is part of a report on the challenges facing the industry. 20 December 2004.

From 1979 to the end of 2003, processing trade grew 243-fold.[30] Since 1995 processing trade has been the most important mode of foreign trade in China. Presently around 50 per cent of China's exports are processed (Figure 4). While there is a deficit under normal trade, China's total trade surplus mainly comes from processing trade – processing of imported materials accounts for three quarters of this trade while the remainder is taken up by the processing of material provided by foreign importers of the eventual finished products.

Figure 4
TREND OF PROCESSING TRADE

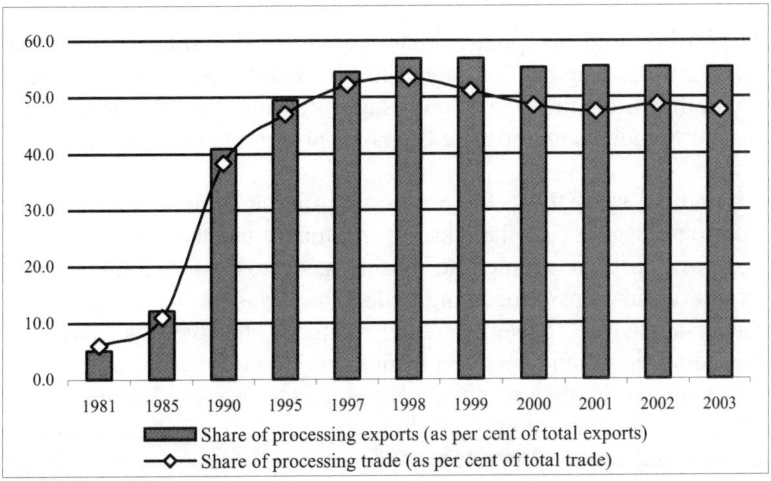

Share of processing exports (as per cent of total exports)
Share of processing trade (as per cent of total trade)

Source: General Administration of Customs of China.

Processing trade was started by companies in Asian NIEs. Most of them were small-scale companies which concentrated on labour-intensive goods, including goods that were anti-dumping intensive and from sunset sectors. This reflects the famous flying geese model of development with early industrializers moving up the production ladder and passing on the traditional sectors to the latecomers. While upgrading their exports from standard basic products into more differentiated products, Hong Kong (China), Japan, Singapore, the Republic of Korea, and Taiwan Province of China transferred some of their traditional and anti-dumping intensive operations into China where labour and infrastructure costs were relatively cheap. This

---

[30] *China Daily*, 15 January 2004: Processing trade to get a boost.

transfer has provided China with the badly needed job opportunities and has also extended product life cycles and profit margins by cutting production costs. This arrangement represents a win-win situation for both China and NIEs. One drawback however is that it is prone to trade disputes. Processing trade requires high import contents for re-exports. According to Messerlin (2002), the

> Five most anti-dumping-intensive HS [harmonized system] sections represent almost 70 per cent of total Chinese imports, opening the possibility that Chinese firms or foreign firms producing in China could table anti-dumping complaints in order to segment world markets... in particular in machinery-electrical equipment and in textiles-clothing.

Messerlin raised one point which deserves further study, namely the question of whether or not China should look into dumping possibilities of those anti-dumping intensive primary and inter-mediary products imported to China for processing or domestic use.

Around the mid-1990s, the processing trade in China entered into a different stage. This has had a profound change on its export compositions but seemed to further accentuate the imbalance in export destinations. Processing trade, which was formerly exclusively labour-intensive, became rather capital-intensive as overseas businesses invested heavily in manufacturing high-tech products such as computer hardware, chemicals and auto parts. Machinery and electronic products now contribute to over half of China's overall exports and about 70 per cent of the entire processing trade volume. This does not mean China's technological level in these products has reached the competitive levels of developed countries. It is rather that the Chinese firms are mainly responsible for the final stages of the production, a division of labour characterized by lower-wage countries for lower-end production, whereas higher-end activities are focused on countries where costs are higher.

According to the Ministry of Commerce, in 2003 around 80 per cent of the processing trade was financed by overseas investors.[31] However, the import contents of these exports are quite high and mostly come from Asian countries. The production of these firms in China, however, relies on imports of machineries to set up the operation, and then imports parts and components for processing and

---

[31] *China Daily*, 15 January 2004: Processing trade to get a boost.

final assembly. While Chinese workers earn a tiny share of the total value of the products in the form of wages, multinational firms are making handsome profits out of these activities. A major source of imports for assembling and re-exporting are from Asian economies. This type of "vertical specialization" of the production process in the Asian region has resulted in China acquiring an increasingly important role in the final assembly stages of a broad range of export commodities. It has also intensified the heavy reliance on United States and European Union markets – the traditional export destinations for Asian exports.

Trade volume between China and the United States accounted for 5.4 per cent of China's GDP in 1997, but rose to 8.95 per cent in 2003. China is the source for the increasing share of goods exported to United States markets. These same goods were those previously produced by Japan, Taiwan Province of China, Singapore, the Republic of Korea and Hong Kong (China). As a result, China has been running big trade deficits with some Asian economies at the same time that it was experiencing a growing surplus with the United States.

In 2003, Japanese exports to China increased by more than 33 per cent. This was a key factor behind the impressive growth performance in Japan. The Republic of Korea's export to China increased by more than 50 per cent. According to a report published by Morgan Stanley in November 2003, exports to China boosted the total export value of Malaysia, Thailand and Singapore by 20 and 30 per cent. Some economists call this trade pattern as the "relocation of deficits". To illustrate this phenomenon, one economist cited electronic exports to the United States as an example.

> The effect of 'relocation of deficits' can best be illustrated by the US trade deficits in electronic products, which increased from US$50.4 billion in 1998 to US$88.8 billion in 2002. This group of products is also important because the US deficit in these products with China came up to as much as US$31.4 billion in 2002, more than one-third of the Sino-US total trade deficit registered in US official figures.... Apparently, US deficits in electronics with China grew by US$17.0 billion during 1998-2002. However, US deficits with Japan decreased by US$7.1 billion and those with Taiwan fell by US$1.5 billion. The 'relocation of deficits' thus constituted more than a half of the increase in Sino-US trade imbalance in electronic products.[32]

---

[32] Hong Kong (China) edition of *China Daily*, 29 December 2003: It's wrong to blame China for the United States trade deficit, by Thomas M. H. Chan.

Thus, although East Asian exports to the United States declined from 40.1 per cent in 1994 to 32.5 per cent in the first half of 2003, China increased its exports to the United States. After a prolonged debate on whether China's trade surplus had taken jobs away from the United States, the Economic Report of the President of the United States released in February 2004 noted that increased trade with China is not contributing to the increased United States trade deficit with the world, as United States imports from other countries had fallen more quickly than the rise in Chinese imports.

The processing trade has been accompanied by sharp increases in imports for processing and re-exports and gave a tremendous boost to China's nominal export value. The value added of processing trade is narrow. With regard to apparel exports

> More than 80 per cent of Chinese apparel exports come from the international joint ventures, which means China is splitting the profits of that business with its foreign partners. China exported 16 billion garments last year, with the export revenue of US$80.48 billion. That indicates China only earns US$5 on each exported piece.[33]

As a result, the increased trade surplus has been far from being proportionate to the increase of the trade volume. The size of current account balance has been declining. Proportionately, in 2002, the weight of the current account surplus over the entire balance of payments has reduced by close to 40 per cent in comparison with the situation in 2000. Trade surplus as a whole also declined. The surplus of merchandise trade, which is a good indication of the international competitiveness of a country, has also been declining.

II.4.   WTO accession condition: Non-market economy status

China's WTO accession protocol states that the country may be treated, on a case-by-case basis, as a non-market economy (NME) for anti-dumping purposes until 2016. The issue of whether or not it is fair to regard China as a NME is not the subject of this paper. However, it needs to be said that being categorized as an NME greatly increases the possibility of a positive dumping ruling and places China at a disadvantage. With this clause in China's accession protocol, the burden to prove "less than normal value" and "material

---

[33] *China Daily*, 6 April 2004: China not the only beneficiary. By Jian Jiangjing.

injury" would be much lighter. As a matter of fact it has also given rise to abuse as production costs can be calculated according to those that are from a surrogate country. Since the surrogate country had not been chosen by the Chinese, it has often transpired that the countries that were chosen were places where material and labour costs were much higher than in China. For example, in an anti-dumping case petitioned by European companies against colour TV sets exported by China to Europe, the European Union Commission selected Singapore as the surrogate country, where labour cost is 20 times higher than in China. In the recent United States anti-dumping investigations against Chinese TV and furniture, India was chosen as the surrogate country in spite of the fact that India is not a big exporter of TVs and furniture. India is at a similar development stage as China but the production costs of small exporters with no scale production are always higher than those of large exporters. Electronic products, in particular, have high start-up costs and achieving economies of scale is important in order to be competitive.

These realities definitely do not lay the foundation for a fair assessment in anti-dumping cases. There are opportunities to manipulate data which in greater likelihood result in a positive ruling of a case. In addition, an assessment of this kind of data could also result in much higher dumping margins, and lead to higher punitive anti-dumping duties. There is also a domino effect as the whole process can be executed relatively easily and the chances of success are high, this in turn leads to a higher level of anti-dumping incidences.

II.5.   Lack of legal capacity to fight against anti-dumping litigations

The lack of legal capacity on the part of Chinese enterprises to respond to anti-dumping investigations abroad is also a factor contributing to the frequency of final anti-dumping measures against Chinese exports. In the past, most of the Chinese exporters were unaware of the anti-dumping process. So when their products were accused of being dumped, their first response was bewilderment and panic. When they learnt of the cost of anti-dumping litigations, they invariably pulled out. As a result, no-response and absentee rulings were quite common, which means affirmative injury ruling was almost a certainty. The lack of qualified staff with good knowledge of the language of the country bringing the case and anti-dumping practice also prevented Chinese enterprises from defending their interests. In this situation the vulnerability of Chinese farmers is unparalleled because most of them are still not aware about dumping and anti-dumping practices. In addition, China had never had any producer/manufacturers' associations before, nor did it have powerful and effective interest groups which can be found in industrialized countries. When each enterprise fought its own battle, their strength definitely could not match their foreign counterparts.

"Echoing" anti-dumping investigations happen very often to China.[34] When a complaint was filed in one country, producers in other countries quickly followed suit. The absence of an immediate response from China after an anti-dumping petition has been filed and the ease with which a positive ruling could be obtained encourages competitors to free ride. This is not only because of fear of trade diversion; it is also a strategic response in order to reduce future competition by eliminating a rival.

II.6. Lack of leverage

The United States and European Union have for many years topped the list of those submitting anti-dumping cases against China. However, as China's exports are highly concentrated in these markets, China does not have much leverage against anti-dumping investigations originating in these markets. Chinese retaliation against anti-dumping activities has been very measured for fear of upsetting major importers, and has thus never constituted a strategic threat to them. The absence of built-in counter-force and credible threat to these markets has placed China at the receiving end of trade restrictive measures. However, with the increase in recent years of both FDI inflows and exports from the United States into China, the situation has, to some degree, been mitigated. China has now even filed anti-dumping cases against the United States.

Prusa (2002) has pointed out that countries generally have significant discretion in the use of anti-dumping law because of the way in which anti-dumping statutes are drafted.[35] Thus, countries and individual industries within countries have learned that they can use the laws to their advantage in a variety of ways. So if politically and strategically

---

[34] Maur (1998).
[35] Prusa (2002:9).

China-bashing during a United States election year is to their advantage, there would be more anti-dumping activities against China. It has been a routine practice to increase trade frictions between the United States and China every election year.

II.7. Developing countries with similar economic development stage

Even though the total number of anti-dumping investigations initiated worldwide has decreased over the past two years, some large developing countries, including China, have increased their use of anti-dumping mechanism. China is also a target of anti-dumping investigations from developing countries. Since 2002 India has replaced the United States as the number one country in launching anti-dumping investigations against Chinese exports. On average, anti-dumping duties from developing countries are higher than those imposed by industrial countries. One example is Mexico which levied punitive tariffs on Chinese footwear as high as 1,105 per cent.

It needs to be pointed out although there is a fundamental difference between anti-dumping activities between those initiated by the developing countries and developed countries. Developing countries have little capacity to engage in FDI to jump anti-dumping. Nor do these countries have latitude to collude with MNEs to squeeze out new rivals. These countries' major concern is to protect domestic producers since it is not possible to rely on tariff protection vis-à-vis widespread trade liberalization. Developing countries neither have the financial capacity to provide domestic support or subsidies to the same degree as the developed countries.

There are two important reasons behind the increasing anti-dumping investigations from developing countries against Chinese exports. Firstly developing countries, with the support of their Governments, become more aware of anti-dumping procedures. Secondly, being at the same stage of development and with exports coming from similar traditional sectors increases the factor that developing countries may be at loggerheads with one another not only in some international but also in domestic markets. Thirdly, the blatant double standard of developed countries in dumping heavily subsidized agricultural products into developing countries and beyond, and their abuse of anti-dumping have made developing countries think they too have to play the same game.

III. CONCLUSION

There have been a number of criticisms about the methodology used to determine dumping, particularly with regard to its opaqueness and the resulting ease of manipulation. For many years, developed countries have been heavy users of anti-dumping activities to protect their sunset industries, and their MNEs have used anti-dumping as a weapon to strengthen monopoly rather than to enhance a "level play field". The inherent weakness and loopholes of anti-dumping laws are among the reasons why China is a target of anti-dumping activities, as it is a new and relatively efficient new rival in the world market. The WTO is currently negotiating within the Negotiation Group on Rules to further clarify and improve the Agreement on Anti-dumping. According to the Doha Ministerial Declaration which was adopted on 14 November 2001, the ongoing negotiation is "aimed at clarifying and improving disciplines" instead of changing the basic concepts and principles, which means anti-dumping activities will continue to have an important impact on international trade.

The present stage of development and development model of the People's Republic of China has determined that in addition to expanding its domestic consumption, trade expansion is as essential for its economic growth. Its trade structure, with the increasing importance of processing trade, may provide the badly needed job opportunities. This may also allow for the relocation of some sunset industrial sectors, and consolidate and expand the existing heavy concentration of export destinations. Although China's export composition has undergone drastic changes, its role as an assembler and final stage producer does place it at a disadvantage when it comes to anti-dumping activities. In the long run, however, it is necessary for China to shift its export products away from anti-dumping-intensive sectors by upgrading export products from standard products into highly differentiated products. The development of China's own brand of products, and undertaking a horizontal production for some important dynamic products can also minimize exposure to foreign anti-dumping charges against Chinese exports and thereby reduce financial losses. In view of the cost of anti-dumping to the economy, it is now time for China to put into place a screening mechanism as permitted by the WTO accession conditions before engaging itself in new processing trade deals.

The extensive safeguard provisions that are included in China's WTO accession commitments could constrain China's export growth. Moreover, intensified anti-dumping activities against Chinese exports will not only be detrimental to China's trade balance; it will also hurt the world. China's track record for trade and economic performance has shown that the benefits of its trade expansion have been distributed much more broadly than have done some earlier NIEs. This is because in a globalizing world, China's exports rely heavily on foreign capital, imports of primary, intermediary and capital goods

REFERENCES

Farrell D, Ghai S and Shavers T (2005). A silver lining in the US trade deficit. *The McKinsey Quarterly*, March 2005, various pages.

Frenkel S (2001). Globalization, athletic footwear commodity chains and employment relations in China. *Organization Studies*, 22(4). ABI.INFORM Global.

Gereffi G, Palpacuer F, and Parisotto A (1999). *Global production and local jobs*. International Labour Office, Geneva, Switzerland.

Harney A (2004). Chinese factories roll out more perks to woo workers. *Financial Times*. 19 March.

Maur JC (1998). *Echoing Anti-dumping Cases, Regulatory Competitors, Imitation and Cascading Protection*. Groupe d'Economie Mondiale & Institute d'Etudes Politiques de Paris.

McCaughrin R (2004). Dispelling trade myths, global economic forum. Morgan Stanley, 5 April. In: http://www.morganstanley.com/ GEFdata/digests/20040405-mon.html#anchor1

Messerlin PA (2002). China in the WTO: anti-dumping and safeguards. *American Economic Review*, 2602.

Miranda J, Torres R and Ruid M (1998). The international use of antidumping: 1987–1997. *Journal of World Trade*, 32(5):5–71.

Nolan P and Zhang Jin (2002). The challenge of globalization for large Chinese firms. *UNCTAD Discussion Papers*, No. 162, July. Geneva, United Nations Conference on Trade and Development.

Pierce RJ Jr (1999). Anti-dumping law as means of facilitating cartelization. *Public Law and Legal Theory Working Paper 002*. Washington DC, George Washington University Law School.

Prusa TJ and Skeath S (2002). Retaliation as an explanation for the proliferation of anti-dumping. *NBER Working Paper 8424*. Cambridge, MA, National Bureau of Economic Research, Inc.

Rumbaugh T and Blancherm N (2004). China: international trade and WTO accession. *IMF Working Paper*, WP/04/36. Washington DC, International Monetary Fund.

United States, International Trade Administration, Department of Commerce. Fact Sheet.

Vandenbussche H, Veugelers R and Belderbos R (1999). Undertakings and anti-dumping jumping FDI in Europe. *Research Report DTEW*, 9941, Leuven.

WTO (2004). World Trade Organization Press Releases, various issues.

Zanardi M (2004). Anti-dumping: what are the numbers to discuss at Doha? *World Economy*, (3).

CHINA'S NEW CONCEPT FOR DEVELOPMENT

Jiyao Bi[1]

INTRODUCTION

In the first 20 years of the 21st century China is entering a new development stage to comprehensively build a prosperous society and to accelerate its modernization drive. China views these two decades as a period of great strategic opportunity which should be pursued vigourously. From an international perspective, peace and development remain the central themes of our era, and China is working to achieve this peaceful environment for development. From a domestic perspective, 25 years of economic reform and opening up have laid a solid basis for development, and China has achieved favourable conditions to accelerate development. However, opportunities are always accompanied by challenges. A key challenge for China is to adopt new thinking and ideas for development and make a new breakthrough in reform, so as to tightly grasp and make a full use of this opportunity to further promote its modernization drive.

I. CHINA'S DEVELOPMENT TRENDS AND ISSUES

China has experienced rapid economic growth since the late 1970s when economic reform and opening policies was initiated. From 1978 to 2004, China's GDP grew by a yearly average of 9.5 per cent, the highest levels of GDP growth in the world. China has successfully maintained its sustained and rapid economic growth in recent years by improving and strengthening macro-control policies. Confronted with the external shocks of the Asian financial crisis of 1997–1998 and the global economic slowdown in 2001–2002, China adopted proactive fiscal policies, a prudent monetary policy as well as restructuring measures to keep rapid economic growth in line with expanding domestic demands. In 2003, China overcame the serious

[1] The opinions expressed in this paper are those of the author and do not necessarily reflect the views of UNCTAD. The author remains solely responsible for any shortcomings in this paper.

impact of the SARS epidemic and recorded 9.3 per cent of economic growth, with GDP totaling US$1.4 trillion; and for the first time GDP per capita surpassing the US$1,000 mark. In order to avoid economic overheating in some sectors and increasing inflationary pressure, especially over-expansion of fixed-assets investment and price hikes of raw materials and farm produce, China promptly shifted its policy focus and took a series of effective macro-control measures to cool down the economy and keep it on a stable and rapid growth track. GDP rose by 9.5 per cent in real terms.

Opening to the outside world has made China increasingly integrated into the world economy. This integration provides markets for China's exports as well as access to sources of capital, technology, expertise, and resources for China's economic development. From 1978 to 2004, China's external trade volume increased 56-fold, with exports and imports increasing from US$9.8 and US$10.9 billion to US$593.4 and US$561.4 billion, respectively. China is now the world's third largest trading nation and the second largest recipient of FDI. From 1984 to 2004, the total stock of FDI in China amounted to US$562.1 billion, with annual FDI inflow increasing from US$2.7 billion to US$60.6 billion over the same period. China has also, in recent years, begun encouraging its enterprises to make investments overseas; by 2004 China's investments overseas were valued at US$37 billion.

The combination of a sustained and rapid economic rate of growth and targeted government programmes, has made it possible for China to significantly improve the living standards of its people and dramatically reduce poverty levels. Rural poverty population declined from 250 million to less than 30 million over the past 25 years. China was ahead of schedule in achieving most of the Millennium Development Goals (MDGs) by 2002, with the target of halving poverty from 1990 level being met. The proportion of the rural population living on an income below US$1 per day fell from 31.3 per cent in 1990 to 11.5 per cent in 2000. Progress has also been made in achieving most of the other MDGs. There are currently 30 million people in rural areas still living in poverty and 20 million urban residents living with minimum living standards. Nevertheless, China has already solved the problem of food and clothing, and generally the people continue to attain better standards of living.

Figure 1
CHINA'S ECONOMIC GROWTH: 1978–2004
(Real GDP growth as per cent of previous year)

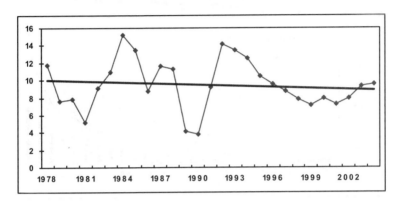

Source: China National Bureau of Statistics.

Figure 2
CHINA AND WORLD GROWTH: 1996–2004
(Real GDP growth as per cent of previous year)

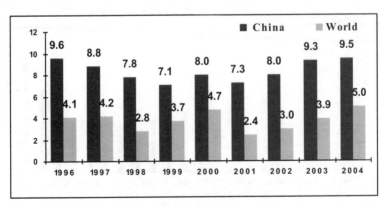

Source: China's National Bureau of Statistics and IMF.

Figure 3
CHINA'S IMPORTS AND EXPORTS: 1978–2004
(Billion of US dollars)

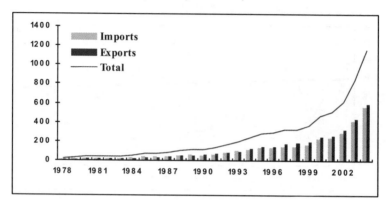

Source: China National Bureau of Statistics.

Figure 4
CHINA'S FDI INFLOWS: 1984–2004
(Billions of US dollars)

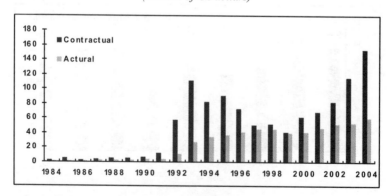

Source: China National Bureau of Statistics.

Together with achieving rapid economic growth and drastic poverty reduction, China has also been experiencing enormous structural transformations. These include shifts from central planning to a market-oriented approach and from agriculture to manufacturing and services as well as from a closed to a globally-integrated economy. While rapid growth and structural changes have solved many problems, China is still facing challenges related to advancing economic and social development due to unfinished economic restructuring and accelerated industrialization and urbanization.

These challenges are mainly reflected as increasing income inequalities, rising urban unemployment and rural underemployment, widening urban-rural gaps in infrastructure, education and public services, growing regional disparities in economic and social development, mounting environmental pressures, potential for macroeconomic instability stemming from incomplete reforms including a weak financial system and low-efficient SOEs, and external risks due to integration into the global economy. Many of these problems cannot be solved by growth alone. Without appropriate policy responses, these problems could deteriorate further. China needs a rethinking of its development strategy, and the adoption of a comprehensive and targeted package of policy measures to meet these challenges and make its development sustainable, both socially and environmentally.

II. CHINA'S DEVELOPMENT STRATEGY FOR MODERNIZATION DRIVE

In the late 1970s, China reversed its development strategy of the previous 30 years and embarked on a programme of economic reform and opening to the outside world. In the early 1980s, China formulated a three-step long-term development strategy to modernize the country: solving the problems of hunger and clothing and lifting most people out of poverty within the 1980s; quadrupling its GDP and per capita GDP as of 1980 and making it possible for people to live a comfortable or a prosperous life by the end of the 20th century; and catching up with the middle-level developed countries by the mid-21st century. In the 1990s, China accelerated its transition from a centrally-planned to a market economy and integration into the global economy, taking a series of important measures such as deepening economic restructuring in almost all the sectors, making the country strong through developing science and education and tapping human resources, implementing sustainable development strategy and western development strategy, strengthening social safety net, and combining bringing in and going global to encourage its economic and social development and opening up. By the end of the 20th century, China had already achieved its strategic development goals of the first two steps in the modernization drive, quadrupling its GDP and per capita GDP by 2000 from 1980 ahead of schedule.

Since the beginning of the 21st century the development of China's economy and society has moved into a new stage of comprehensively building a prosperous society and of speeding up the process of modernization. China's third stage of implementing its development strategy for modernization consists of establishing an ambitious national objective to concentrate on comprehensively building a prosperous society in the first 20 years of the 21st century, bringing more benefits to more than one billion of its citizens. GDP is expected to quadruple from the level of US$1.1 trillion reached in 2000, which implies an average growth rate of 7.2 per cent per year, and per capita GDP of US$3,000 in the final year, compared to US$940 today. Consequently, by 2020 the average living standard in China is expected to reach the level found today in the upper middle-income developing countries, as defined by the World Bank. In addition to rapid economic growth and increasing average incomes, comprehensively building a prosperous society also involves – explicitly or implicitly – other dimensions of China's overall economic and social development, and includes: optimizing economic structure; enhancing efficiency and productivity; consolidating national strength and international competitiveness; completing market-oriented economic reform; making the economy more dynamic and open; advancing both industrialization and urbanization; narrowing the urban-rural gap and regional disparities; improving the social security system; creating sufficient employment; strengthening education, science, technology and innovation, as well as public health; increasing the capability of sustainable development; and constructing a harmonious society, etc. In brief, comprehensively building a prosperous society will significantly advance China's economic and social development, and will lay a solid foundation to achieve the third-step of the strategic goal of the modernization drive.

While establishing the ambitious objective to build a prosperous society in a comprehensive manner, China views the first two decades of the 21st century as an important period with strategic opportunities that must be seized to accelerate its economic and social development.

Taking a global perspective, it is clear that strategic patterns are changing rapidly and profoundly, and that peace and development have kept their place as the central themes of our era. It is also clear that basic political and economic trends around the world are favourable to China's modernization drive. The intensified globalization of economic activities, rapid progress of science and technology, as well as global adjustments of industrial structures, are providing many opportunities for China to advance its industrialization drive and sustain its development by participating in globalization and giving full play to its comparative advantages such as abundant low-cost labour resources and huge market potential. However, as China has become further integrated into the world economy following its accession to the WTO and more dependent on external markets and resources, a variety of external shocks can more easily affect China's macroeconomic stability. It is imperative for China to incorporate opening policies with development strategy more effectively, so as to make better use of both external and domestic markets and resources.

From a domestic perspective, it is clear that China has many favourable conditions for sustaining its rapid development. A number of impediments stand in the way of development as well. With per capita GDP exceeding US$1,000, China has entered a golden development period and, as shown by international experiences, a period in which various contradictions arouse. With the acceleration of industrialization, China needs to continuously optimize and upgrade its industrial structure in order to shape a balanced industrial pattern with hi-tech industries taking the lead, supported by basic industries and manufacturing, and complemented by the overall development of various services. Rapid urbanization and the large number of migrants from rural to urban areas also means that China needs to also change the dual nature of its urban-rural economic and social structures and related management systems and institutions as soon as possible.

The ever-expanding regional disparities call for coordination of regional development by means of more balanced development strategies and better targeted policy measures to support less developed regions. Increasing pressures on the environment and natural resources as well as lagging development in public services such as education, health care, and social security are factors that are forcing China to accelerate a transformation in the processes of economic growth in order to achieve overall progress in social development. With market mechanisms playing an increasing and significant role in economic activities, China needs to strengthen and improve macro-control and further perfect its market economic system, so as to maintain macroeconomic stability and sustain a rapid economic growth. While various social contradictions are emerging and becoming acute, China must also establish a long-term effective mechanism to encourage social harmony, coordinate various interests, protect legal rights and maintain social stability.

In order to deal with various contradictions appropriately, meet the severe challenges ahead as well as make its economic and social development sustainable for the benefit of more people, China has to adopt new thinking on its concept for development, explore a suitable road for development, and improve its strategies for development by summing up both its own and international experiences and lessons of development practices. For this purpose, China proposes a new concept based on science to guide its economic and social development while comprehensively building a prosperous society.

The new concept for development gives priority to human development, emphasizes environmental and socially sustainable development, and insists on an overall and coordinated development of the economy, society and the people. The new concept for development is based on science, and reflects the evolution of China's thinking and its understanding of development. The new concept is also based on the distillation of China's experiences and lessons with the development process up to the present day, all of which will be incorporated into China's development strategy and related policies.

III. CHINA'S NEW CONCEPT FOR DEVELOPMENT AND ITS IMPLICATIONS

The concept for development is the general perspective and fundamental viewpoint on the essence, purpose, contents and requirements of development. Different concepts for development will result in different paths and modes of development and development strategies; and these results will in turn bear upon fundamental and overall impacts on development practices. Economic development is the core essence for any concept for development.

China's new development concept is proposed on the basis of science and the distillation of development experiences and lessons both at home and abroad. It is a scientific concept of progress towards a comprehensive, coordinated, and sustainable development path which upholds the people first principle. Fundamental to this scientific concept, in line with the principle of putting the people first, is to achieve overall human development – to plan and encourage development of the fundamental interests for culture and leisure, health and security and to meet their increasing consumption needs.

Comprehensive and sustained economic and social development entails focus on economic, political and cultural construction in a comprehensive manner in order to achieve sustained and sound economic development, as well as overall social progress. A coordinated development also involves achieving an equilibrium between urban-rural and regional development; economic and social development; the harmonious development between man and his environment; domestic development and opening up. A sustainable development seeks to encourage a balanced co-existence between mankind and nature by establishing this equilibrium between economic and social development on the one hand and on the other with the various forces at play – the people, the resources and environment.

In order to build a prosperous society and drive forward modernization, China should seize all available opportunities. As a large developing country, China has to maintain rapid economic growth over a long period; otherwise, there is the risk of being unable to provide a better standard of living for its people, let alone achieve progress elsewhere. However, a rapid rate of growth cannot be pursued at the expense of quality and efficiency. Rapid economic development should be based on optimizing economic structures and enhancing quality and efficiency. China's economic growth has been fuelled by increasing inputs and expanding investment over a long period of time – at the cost of large expenses in resources with its corollary impact on environment. Consequently, China must take a new road to industrialization and give more emphasis on science and technology, high economic efficiency, low consumption of resources, less damage to the environment, and leveraging its advantages in human resources. China also needs to change the way its economic growth has been handled and promote a strategic adjustment of economic structure, and achieve rapid growth based on technological progress and productivity increases.

Coordinating urban-rural development is determined by China's unique national condition of large population living in the rural areas. The difficulty of comprehensively building a prosperous society and driving modernization forward lies in the rural rather than urban areas. While agriculture only accounted for about 14.6 per cent of China's GDP in 2003, the country's rural population accounts for 59.5 per cent of the total population, and 49.5 per cent of China's labour force is active in agriculture. China's arable land only accounts for 13 per cent of its territory, and has 40 per cent less arable land per capita than anywhere else in the world. With more people and less arable land in rural areas, its comparative advantage is lower in agriculture.

Greater population levels, less arable land in rural areas, and a lower comparative advantage in agriculture, among a number of other systemic and policy reasons have meant that investment have excessively been concentrated in cities and industry for a considerable period of time. This has led to slower development in rural areas, not only on an economic level but also on many other sectors such as education, science and technology, culture and health care, etc. The gap between urban-rural areas has grown increasingly larger, particularly in relation to economic and social development and income inequalities. Without development in rural areas, the living standard of farmers cannot not be raised, which will inevitably affect consumption upgrading and market expansion, and will ultimately hold back China's economic development. In comprehensively building a prosperous society,

China must accelerate the transformation of its dual urban-rural economic and social structure, attach high importance to rural economic and social development, and quicken the pace of urbanization, so as to encourage coordinated development between rural and urban areas.

In general, a concept of "Five Coordination", i.e., coordination of urban-rural development, regional development, economic and social development, human development and the nature, and domestic development and opening up further clarify the guiding principles for China's reform and development in this new century and stage. These five enrich the contents of the scientific concept for development and provide cutting-points for putting the scientific concept for development into practices. By focusing on the "Five Coordination" and giving due consideration to various interests involved, China is thus able to achieve a comprehensive, coordinated, and sustainable development while putting people first.

Coordinating regional development is of the utmost importance for a country like China with its vast territory and large population. From the beginning of the period of economic reform and opening up, China took a series of preferential and flexible policies to accelerate the development of its coastal areas. With the supporting policies and location advantages, the east coast has taken a lead in development, and has contributed significantly to the sustained and rapid economic growth of the whole country. At the same time, regional disparities have also grown. The interior areas were lagging behind not only in economic and social development but in the development of physical infrastructure such as roads, railways, power, telecommunications and water supply as well. In order to address these regional disparities and achieve a balanced development, China has taken a series of development strategies to guide and coordinate regional developments. In 1999, China launched a Western Region Development Strategy to accelerate economic and social development in the less developed western provinces, with a focus on improving infrastructure, protecting the environment, encouraging private sector investment, and creating conditions for the proliferation of a wide range of economic activities based on the market economy. The western region, which includes 12 provinces, occupies 71 per cent of China's territory, and has a population and GDP which accounts for 29 per cent and 17 per cent, respectively, of the whole country.

Economic and social development indicators such as per capita GDP, urbanization ratio, primary enrollment ratio, life expectancy, and poverty ratio are significantly lower in relation to national levels. Without development in the western region, China could not successfully achieve its goal to comprehensively build a prosperous society and advance modernization. After the implementation of the Coast Opening Strategy and the Western Region Development Strategy, China has recently begun to implement the Northeast Old Industrial Base Development Strategy, aiming to further coordinate development among various regions.

Coordinating economic and social development is an inevitable requirement of comprehensively building a prosperous society in China. Sustained and rapid economic development has lifted millions of people out of poverty and solved the problem of food and clothing for the Chinese people. However, social problems such as unemployment, urban poverty, healthcare, social security and protection for rights and interests have emerged and become acute in the process of economic development, structural adjustment, and systemic reforms. Compared with its rapid economic development, China has lagged behind in the reform and development on education, science and technology, public healthcare, social security system, and other social services and could not meet the increasing demands of the people. In comprehensively building a prosperous society, it is imperative for China to accelerate social development in all its aspects.

Coordinating harmonious development between man and nature is an urgent task for China in order to achieve sustainable development. As was proved by practices in China and abroad, the massive scale of development, natural resources utilization along with industrialization and technical progress has not only brought huge benefits to mankind. These activities have also brought serious damage and pollution to the environment and its natural resources. Environmental protection has become an increasingly important preoccupation and clean production, green economy, recycling economy, to mention a few among other methods aimed at environmental protection, has gained in popularity worldwide. China's accelerating industrialization and advancing modernization, its large population, low resources endowment, and a vulnerable ecosystem has exerted increasing pressures on the environment and natural resources and has threatened China's sustainable development.

In order to achieve coordinated development between the economy, society, population, resources and the environment, China needs to live its economic growth efficiently: to advocate healthy life-styles and consumption behaviour, actively engage in economizing resources and strengthen ecosystem construction and environmental protection so as to increase the potentials for a sustained development.

Coordinating domestic development and opening up is an inevitable choice for China to make good use of both internal and external markets and resources and to increasingly enhance international competitiveness. The globalization of various economic activities is a general trend of the world economy. Upon accession to the WTO, China has become further integrated into the world economy, with international competition becoming internalized and domestic compe-tition internationalized. Because China depends on international markets and resources more heavily, fluctuations in the world economy also affect China's economic performance more easily. In order to sustain its rapid economic development and to increasingly enhance its international competitiveness, China has had to insist on opening policies. Not only should domestic development and reform have international environments taken into consideration; an opening to the outside world should also serve the requirements of domestic development. By fully participating in globalization, China will not only continue to take in foreign capital, advanced technology, as well as expertise to develop hi-tech industry and transform traditional industry. China will also go abroad to expand regional economic cooperation and tap international markets and resources.

As a large and populous country, China's long-term development should be based on expanding domestic markets and demands. However, these development goals cannot be achieved in isolation. The key question is how to coordinate domestic development with opening up as China is increasingly integrated into the global economy.

IV. CHINA'S POLICY STRATEGY FOR IMPLEMENTING THE NEW CONCEPT FOR DEVELOPMENT

The new concept for development is a guiding principle for China's economic and social development while achieving its goal of comprehensively building a prosperous society in the first two decades of the 21st century. To put the new concept for development into practice, China needs to reshape its development strategies and related policies, especially focusing more on the following aspects:

Sustaining rapid growth based on quality and efficiency

Although China has successfully maintained rapid growth and stability in recent years by improving macroeconomic management, the quality and efficiency of this growth are still a matter of concern. The resource-intensive and less efficient growth pattern characterized by a high input/output ratio, low employment content and high environmental cost to a large extent results from unfinished economic reform and defective economic structure. The acceleration of economic reform and focus on breaking up local protectionism, facilitating migration, commercializing the banking sector, opening administratively monopolized sectors to private investors, reducing government intervention in resources pricing, gradually liberalizing interest rates, among other factors, will improve efficiency of resource allocation and sustain rapid growth through domestic market integration and freer flow of goods and services, capital, and resources as well as technology diffusion. Accelerating the development of the services sector and building an enabling environment for the private sector will create more jobs. Stricter measures for environmental protection and incentives for clean production will reduce damage to the environment.

While enhancing the quality and efficiency of growth, macro-economic policies should be well designed according to changing economic conditions to maintain rapid growth and macroeconomic stability. China has become a market-based economy, with most prices determined by market forces and enterprises responsible for their own profits and losses. China's macro-control measures should therefore gradually be shifted towards standardized fiscal and monetary policies such as regulating interest rates and the taxation ratio and reducing direct intervention of governments in economic activities. These control measures should make the economy grow more robustly.

Reducing urban-rural inequalities

China has taken a series of policy measures to increase the income of farmers and encourage rural development. These measures include reducing the fiscal burden on farmers by (i) restructuring rural taxation by introducing tax-for-fee reform, (ii) abolishing agricultural tax, (iii) granting direct subsidies to grain planters, (iv) increasing government expenditure on rural education, science and technology, public health, and infrastructure, and (v) helping rural surplus labor find jobs in non-farming sectors. To contain the widening urban-rural gap, an integrated approach should be adopted. As around 50 per cent of the labour force is engaged in agriculture, improving the performance of agriculture represents the most direct way to reduce urban-rural inequalities. Moreover, given the available arable land and irrigation constraints, the agricultural development should focus on increasing farm productivity, diversifying crop plantation, and strengthening comprehensive grain production capacity.

While increasing government investment in rural infrastructure such as roads, electricity, and telecommunication, China is also taking steps to rebuild rural financial systems, i.e. restructuring rural credit cooperatives and establishing various agricultural services networks such as farm produce processing, storage and transportation, marketing and distribution, as well as technical and information services. All these are intended to help farmers increase their income through improved financial and producer services.

An effective way to increase farmers' income is to reduce the number of farmers. This will involve many aspects of institutional reforms such as creating more jobs in non-farm sectors, eliminating discriminatory policies to migrant workers, providing training and employment services. To be able to cope with rapidly increasing migrants from the rural to urban areas, urban housing and infrastructure and the development of an urban social security system as well is envisaged.

Addressing regional disparities

Regional disparities in China result from different natural endowments, geographic factors and policy effects. China's recent development strategy has placed more emphasis on a balanced growth pattern focused on accelerating development in the lagging geographic regions, especially selected provinces in the interior and western parts of the country.

The Western Region Development Strategy that was launched in 1999 has borne fruit; it has improved infrastructure such as transportation, communications and power. The Strategy has helped to protect the natural environment through conversion of marginal lands into forests and water resources management, thus laying a foundation for development. However, the effects of this Strategy have had a negligible effect on creating an attractive climate for foreign and private investment; on the conditions for dynamic activities based on market economy; and on narrowing coastal/interior income inequality. Unattractive business environments and high transport costs as well as artificial low resources pricing are still impediments to the development of the interior and western regions. Additional supportive policy measures should focus on improving investment and the business climate to attract investment, invigorate local economic activities to create more jobs, reduce transport costs by bringing in more competition, give more autonomy in resources pricing and standardize intergovernmental transfer payments.

The Northeast Old Industrial Base Development Strategy that was recently launched seems to have learnt some lessons from the Western Region Development Strategy and had placed more emphasis on mechanisms and institutional innovations such as deepening SOE reform, a pilot value-added tax transformation and socialization of social security. These all have been found to be more effective in encouraging local economic development.

Addressing regional disparities is a long-term challenge in China. The specific strategies and policies need to be more clearly targeted and better designed. Further, effective policies to reduce regional disparities should be made compatible with promoting national economic growth.

Strengthening social security system

As China is experiencing a rapid transition into a market-based economy and its accompanying enormous structural transformations, an urgent task now facing China is to strengthen its social security system which is an essential component of a market economy. China's current social security system covers only a small part of the population, mainly urban employees in SOEs and collective enterprises. This leaves most of the population unprotected – employees in private and foreign-funded enterprises, the migrant workers, and farmers. The system also suffers from financial weaknesses, decentralized management, segmented urban-rural schemes and imperfect laws and regulations. The general direction is to establish a suitable social security system compatible with economic development levels in China. The objective is to build a system that is independent of enterprises and institutions, diversified fund sources, standardized protection regime and socialized management and services.

The basic principles incorporate extensive coverage, appropriate standards, social pooling combined with individual account, and basic protection supplemented by other social insurances. China is currently in the process of strengthening its social security system by focusing on urban pension, unemployment benefits, basic medical insurance, industrial injury insurance, and minimum living standard scheme. Various social security schemes are also being tested in selected rural areas. Priorities in social security reform include extending social security in urban areas by widening coverage and to include migrants, centralizing the financing and provision of social security at the provincial level, and establishing income maintenance and basic insurance schemes in rural areas.

Making growth environmentally sustainable

Despite remarkable progress to improve the environment over the past 15 years, China is still facing many challenges such as air pollution, water pollution, solid waste pollution, land degradation and desertification. And continued economic growth is still exerting increasing pressures on the environment and natural resources.

To make growth environmentally sustainable, China needs to enhance public awareness and participation in environmental protection and insist on a sustainable development strategy. The legal and institutional systems for environmental protection and natural resources management should be improved and strengthened, including a nationwide system of monitoring, recording, and reporting the discharge of pollutants. While strengthening regulatory system and improving law enforcement, China needs to make great use of market-based instruments in environmental protection, such as providing economic incentives to the development of renewable energy, internalizing social costs for coal-fired power generation, opening pollution treatment sectors to private investors, granting investment tax credit to enterprises applying clean production lines, and increasing charges on emissions. The Government should continue to play a leading role in environmental protection, including putting more resources into environmental protection and ecosystem rehabilitation and implementing stricter evaluation on the environmental impacts of construction projects. Environmental protection, economic development and poverty reduction are inextricably linked. Thus, growth that is environmentally friendly requires more comprehensive policies and integrated approaches.

In general, adopting and implementing the new concept for development involve arduous works on many aspects. China needs to rethink its various specific development strategies and policies and reshape them with the new concept for development incorporated.

V. CONCLUSION

China's remarkable achievements on sustained economic development, large-scale poverty reduction, as well as its gradual transition to a market economy have been admired by international society. As indicated by the Asian Development Bank in its Country Strategy and Program (2004–2006) for China, "When the economic history of the last part of the 20th century is written, the People's Republic of China will be recognized as one of the world's great development success stories." In its first assessment report on China's progress in attaining the MDGs launched in 2003, the UNDP also praises China for having made enormous progress toward achieving its MDGs.

Despite its remarkable achievements in economic and social development, China is also facing many new challenges, some of these have been raised on a number of occasions by international organizations such as the United Nations Country Team in China, the World Bank, and Asian Development Bank; these challenges include how to address income inequalities and regional disparities, how to make development socially and environmentally sustainable, how to complete reform agendas, how to tackle the social, economic and fiscal risks that may threaten future growth and distributional performance.

China has full understanding of its problems and challenges ahead to comprehensively build a prosperous society and advance its modernization drive. The new concept for development has been chosen in order to tackle existing problems and meet future challenges; it also represents China's new thinking on development. By putting it into practice and incorporating it in specific strategies and policies, China will be able to make new progress in sustaining economic and social development.

REFERENCES

ADB (2003). *Country Strategy and Program (2004–2006): The People's Republic of China.* Asian Development Bank, Manila.

Jiang Zemin (2002). Building a well-off society in an all-round way, opening up a new prospect for the socialist cause with Chinese characteristics. Political report delivered to the 16th National Congress of the Communist Party of China, Beijing.

United Nations Country Team in China (2004). *Millennium Development Goals: China's Progress 2003.* Office of the United Nations Resident Coordinator in China, Beijing.

Wen Jiabao (2004). Firmly establishing and earnestly implementing the scientific concept for development. Speech given at the closing ceremony of the workshop in Central Party School, Beijing.

World Bank (2003). *China: Promoting Growth with Equality. Country Economic Memorandum*, Report No. 24169-CHA. Washington DC.

World Bank (2004). *China: An Evaluation of World Bank Assistance.* Call order 338.910951 CH. Washington DC.

FDI IN CHINA:
TRENDS AND MACROECONOMIC CHALLENGES

Sebastian Dullien[1]

Abstract

This paper examines the role of FDI in the Chinese economic development process of the past decades and tries to predict imminent trends and their consequences. It is found that the type of FDI prevalent will most likely shift from the primarily efficiency-seeking kind producing for markets abroad towards the more market-seeking kind both in manufacturing sectors hitherto closed to foreign competitions and in service sectors. This trend will pose problems as market-seeking FDI proposes fewer benefits than efficiency-seeking FDI as the new kind of FDI is more likely to crowd out domestic firms and investment. Moreover, market-seeking FDI tends to be a burden on the current account in the medium and long term as companies repatriate their earnings. This might force China to rely on capital imports to finance domestic absorption and make the country more vulnerable for currency crises.

INTRODUCTION

Within 25 years, China has developed from being an almost completely closed economy to becoming the world's second largest recipient country of foreign direct investment (FDI) in the late 1990s. With FDI inflows to the United States slumping in 2002, China even managed to become the largest FDI recipient in that year. While FDI to the United States recovered in 2004, one thing is undisputable: FDI has played a significant role in the Chinese economy in recent decades. Especially in China's booming manufacturing export sector, foreign investment has been very strong. Foreign firms have invested heavily in China to benefit from cheap labour costs. More than half of China's exports are now produced by foreign-owned firms. A large proportion of these exports is in assembly trade, in which foreign

[1] The opinions expressed in this paper are those of the author and do not necessarily reflect the views of UNCTAD. The author remains solely responsible for any shortcomings in this paper.

firms bring parts to China for final assembly and later re-exports. Foreign firms have used this mechanism to help China gain shares in world markets, particularly important at a time when China's domestic level of development in sectors such as electronics and appliances would not yet have allowed for.

However, with real wages and incomes increasing and a slight rise in inflation leading to a real appreciation of the Chinese renminbi since the end of the 1990s, the question is how long this heavy reliance on FDI in the export sector is sustainable. As relative unit labour costs start to rise in China[2] investors might find other Asian countries more attractive for efficiency-seeking FDI in a not too distant future. At the same time, China has also agreed to open domestic markets, e.g. in financial services to foreign companies. This will most likely lead to more foreign direct investment in activities aimed to provide for the domestic Chinese market. Thus, a shift from efficiency-seeking to market-seeking FDI (meaning that firms invest in a country to gain access to domestic markets) might be in the making. This shift might be further amplified by the global trend towards FDI in services as has been described in the *World Investment Report 2004* under the heading *The Shift Towards Services* (UNCTAD 2004b).

The interesting question now is what this change from a low-income economy, in which foreigners invest to profit from cheap labour to a middle-income economy in which foreigners compete for market shares implies for China, and where there may be obstacles in the way of a continued and smooth economic development process. This paper will attempt to answer these questions. The further analysis is structured as follows: section I will briefly outline the trends in Chinese FDI inflows; section II will examine the role FDI has played in the spectacular growth performance since the mid-1990s; section III will examine recent and imminent changes in China's inward FDI; section IV will diagnose potential problems and section V proposes possible remedies.

---

[2] See, for example, the unit-labour cost based real effective exchange rate in China (Dullien 2004b).

I. FDI IN CHINA: STYLIZED TRENDS

China's Government began to allow foreign direct investment into China very early on in the reform process. In 1979, the National People's Congress passed the Equity Joint Venture Law and thereby legislated for the first time an – albeit careful – opening of the Chinese economy. However, until 1986, foreign investment was "permitted" rather than "encouraged" (Huang 2003); however, after 1986 FDI in some, mainly export-oriented and technologically advanced sectors, was actively promoted.

FDI only became highly significant for the Chinese economy until the mid-1990s; it began to grow strongly after a number of bilateral investment treaties were signed in 1992 (including the important memorandum of understanding with the United States on a number of issues ranging from market access to intellectual property rights protection). An amplifying factor was the concurrent strong real depreciation of the Chinese currency which made producing in China relatively more attractive (UNCTAD 2004a). From 1991 to 1994, the share of FDI in the country's gross fixed capital formation increased from 3.9 to more than 17 per cent (Figure 1),[3] FDI's share in GDP grew from 1.5 to 6.7 per cent over the same time period.

From 1994 onwards, the significance of FDI for the Chinese economy declined again, with FDI amounting to 11.2 per cent of gross fixed capital formation and 4.2 per cent of GDP in 2002. However, this decline was not brought about by an absolute fall in FDI, but by a strong growth of the Chinese economy and domestic investment in China. From 1994 to 2002, real GDP increased by roughly 90 per cent, while annual FDI inflow adjusted by the investment deflator increased by 40 per cent – still a significant increase, but below GDP growth. Moreover, the decline of the share of FDI in gross fixed capital formation hides the importance of foreign enterprises in some sectors: As a share of non-government

---

[3] Of course, FDI does not transmit one-to-one into fixed capital formation as sometimes only the ownership of assets is transferred. However, this indicator gives an impression of the importance of FDI relative to overall investment.

Figure 1
FDI AS SHARE OF FIXED CAPITAL FORMATION IN CHINA

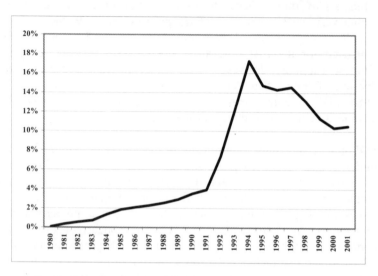

Source: Estimations based on UNCTAD and World Bank data.

and non-state-owned-enterprise investment, FDI still amounts to more than 20 per cent (Figure 2).[4] The share of exports originating in foreign-owned firms even reached more than 50 per cent in 2003. Finally, FDI stocks account for a significant share of the domestic capital stock. Estimations hint that roughly 14 per cent of the capital stock is owned by foreign companies (Figure 3).

If we take a look at recent FDI developments by sector (Table 1), we can see that manufacturing received almost three quarters of overall FDI in 2001.[5] Moreover, FDI in manufacturing also experienced the largest increase, both in absolute terms and in percentage terms since the late 1990s.

---

[4] The number is derived as follows: Inward FDI stock in dollars is converted into 1990 Yuan using the investment deflator. This number is set into relation to an estimated capital stock using the perpetual inventory methods from Chinese investment data going back to the 1960s. While this method might not be quite accurate given the large technological changes in China's investment during the past decade, it seems to be the best proxy available.
[5] Unfortunately, more recent data is not available.

Figure 2
FDI AS SHARE OF PRIVATE INVESTMENT IN CHINA

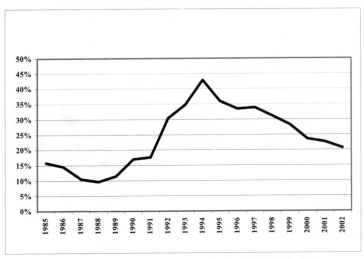

Source: Estimations based on UNCTAD and World Bank data.

Figure 3
SHARE OF FDI IN CHINA'S CAPITAL STOCK

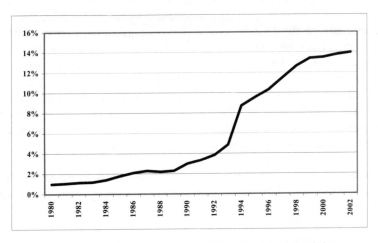

Source: Estimations based on UNCTAD and World Bank data.

Table 1
SINGLE SECTORS' SHARES OF FDI
(In per cent)

Sector	1998	1999	2000	2001
Farming, foresting, etc.	1.4	1.8	1.7	2.6
Mining and quarrying	1.3	1.4	1.4	0.9
Manufacturing	56.2	56.0	63.4	71.3
Electric power, gas & water	6.8	9.2	5.5	3.1
Construction	4.5	2.3	2.2	2.7
Transportation, storage, posts and telecom services	3.6	3.8	2.5	1.3
Wholesale and retail trade and catering	2.6	2.4	2.1	2.0
Real estate management	14.1	13.9	11.4	7.3
Social services	6.5	6.3	5.4	6.3
Health care, sports and social welfare	0.2	0.4	0.3	0.2
Education, culture and arts	0.2	0.2	0.1	0.1
Other	2.5	2.4	3.9	2.1

Source: Chinese Statistical Office.

However, the high growth rate of manufacturing FDI hides the fact that foreign investments have not only been efficiency-seeking and thus sought at producing for export. A certain (but unfortunately not quantifiable) share of FDI has already been set aside to provide for the growing Chinese domestic market. For example, all of the investments made by foreign automobile companies have been made to provide for the Chinese market and circumvent high import duties of sometimes more than 100 per cent. This can be seen in the fact that Chinese exports (both from domestic and foreign-owned firms) in automobiles are currently negligible. Even though some analysts believe in an upturn in Chinese car exports in the near future, persistent high costs and the low quality of Chinese car production suggests that global car companies would rather use production bases outside China for exports to the world market in the coming years.[6]

Moreover, all the investments in service sectors such as wholesale, retail, real estate, but also in construction and energy production are

---

[6] An exception might be some limited exports in third low-income markets.

clearly aimed at providing for local customers and firms and must therefore be classified as market-seeking.

Unfortunately, it is hard to distinguish exactly how much FDI has been efficiency-seeking and how much has been market-seeking as it is impossible to distinguish between the two types of FDI in manufacturing from the aggregate data. The fact that the aggregate wage sum has been growing rather strongly and real incomes in urban areas have also been increasing briskly (albeit from a very low and competitive level),[7] would lead us to expect that the trend has rather been towards a larger share of FDI of the market-seeking type in total FDI, particularly in recent years.

II. THE ROLE OF FDI IN CHINA'S DEVELOPMENT

Given the enormous weight of FDI in the Chinese economy, a central question is what role this investment has played in China's growth performance in the past decade. Among economists, net benefits of FDI are highly disputed. While proponents argue that foreign direct investment bring about an injection of productive resources into the host economy including new technology which increases the rate of technological progress in the host economy and might lead to additional investment ("crowding in"), opponents warn that by competing for scarce resources such as qualified labour, natural resources, but also market opportunities and market demand, foreign investment might actually replace and thus crowd out domestic investment.[8]

II.1. Theoretical arguments in favour and against FDI

Proponents base their arguments on two points: First, they claim that FDI gives countries access to resources they could otherwise not obtain, one example of this is foreign exchange. If a country is not able to obtain the foreign exchange necessary to buy capital goods either by exporting or by borrowing in international financial markets, so the argument runs, FDI might be an option to gain access

---

[7] See the figures in ILO's *LABORSTA* database.
[8] For a discussion of arguments for and against FDI with a special focus on services, see also chapter III in UNCTAD 2004.

to these funds. Second, proponents also maintain that FDI leads to a spillover of advanced technologies and knowledge from foreign investments into the host country. According to this view, foreign firms are demonstrating new technologies, providing technological assistance to their local suppliers and customers, and are training workers who may subsequently work in domestic firms (Kokko 1994). Moreover, the advanced technology that these imported intermediate goods may contain could spill over into the domestic economy, along the lines of the endogenous growth model of Bayoumi et al. (1999). In addition, foreign firms may have a wealth of knowledge on access to world markets which the host country does not have, or could only acquire slowly, and which provides local suppliers with income-generating possibilities. Finally, the additional competition induced by foreign firms might also force domestic firms to become more efficient, forcing them to innovate.

Skeptics, on the other hand, argue that foreign firms may simply push domestic firms out of the market as they are more technologically advanced. Even a partial crowding out might be a problem as it is not evident whether the foreign-owned firms are as beneficial for domestic technological progress as similarly successful domestic ones. First, foreign firms might use domestic upstream and down-stream production networks to a much lesser extent than domestic firms. Thus, a partial crowding out in one stage might choke off investment and thereby potential income and technology generation at other stages. Second, there are some indications that research and development activities in multinational enterprises remain heavily concentrated in their headquarters (Dunning 1998). Thus, a partial crowding out of some activity by a foreign affiliate might reduce technology enhancing research and development activity in the host country.

Finally, if FDI is market-seeking, it might have adverse balance-of-payments-effects later on (Nunnenkamp and Spatz 2003). As the foreign company will try to repatriate (part of) its earnings later, the inflow of FDI will be followed by an outflow of profit incomes in the future. As this profit outflow constitutes a debit in the current account of the balance of payments, this might weaken the external position and might even lead to a deficit in the current account, making further inflows of foreign capital necessary. Considered in the context of volatile private capital flows, this may increase the risk of balance of payments crisis in the future, which may in turn inflict serious damage on growth prospects.

II.2. Empirical evidence on FDI

The overall empirical evidence as to whether the net effect of FDI is positive or negative on the host country's economic performance is inconclusive, both across and within countries. While older studies such as De Gregorio (1992) find evidence for the positive growth effects of FDI, particularly in favourable environments, studies on the impact on micro-data such as Aitken and Harrison (1999) do not find evidence for any positive effect of FDI. Moreover, Carkovic and Levine (2002) seriously question the robustness of older macroeconomic studies as they do not take into account a possible simultaneity bias, country-specific effects, and lagged variables. They find that using modern econometric techniques, a significantly positive effect of FDI on economic growth cannot be found. Nunnenkamp and Spatz (2003) confirm the finding that a general link between FDI and economic growth cannot be established. However, they identify a number of host country and investment characteristics which determine whether the effect of certain FDI is positive or negative. For example, according to their study, FDI in manu-facturing has significant positive effects as long as it is efficiency-seeking, but not if it is market-seeking.

For a single country, especially in a country such as China that has experienced lots of structural changes due to a transformation to a market-based economy, it is impossible to empirically determine the net effect of past foreign direct investment. However, theoretical considerations can give a hint as to which partial effects might have had a significant effect on growth.

The first question would be whether China needed FDI in order to bridge some "foreign exchange gap" (ADB 2004) between the foreign exchange it could earn itself and the amount it needed in order to import capital goods necessary for its economic development. For the country as a whole, it is plainly evident that, from the time FDI really took off in China in the mid-1990s, the country was not short of foreign exchange: Since 1994, China achieved a surplus in the current account balance, thus earning more foreign exchange with its exports than were necessary to pay for the imports. Lately, the country's problem has even become an excess than a lack of foreign reserves, with a net accumulation of reserves of more than US$200 billion in 2004 alone (an equivalent of roughly 12.5 per cent of GDP and way above FDI inflows).

However, what is true on an aggregate level does not necessarily hold on a micro-level. As Huang (2001) argues, private Chinese firms have for a long time been disadvantaged in their access to foreign exchange. These problems have eased with attempts of Chinese monetary authorities to promote foreign exchange outflows in 2003.[9] However, according to the World Bank's Business Environment Survey of 2000, obtaining access to long-term finance is still considered to be the greatest single obstacle for Chinese companies doing business in China. The banking system still seems to be geared towards the needs of State-Owned Enterprises (SOEs) and only makes very small loans to privately-owned domestic firms. This situation might effectively amount to a lack of access to foreign exchange at the micro-level and could be cured by FDI inflows as the foreign parent companies usually have access to the originating country's banking system and can thus provide their affiliates with foreign exchange. Thus, the FDI inflow might alleviate problems private firms have with the domestic banking sector. However, the question of whether this effect could not have been easier achieved by reforming the banking sector is open to debate.

Another question is whether domestic Chinese firms have been crowded out by the strong FDI inflow, or whether FDI has triggered an increase in domestic investment ("crowding in"). Agosin and Mayer (2000) do not find evidence for any crowding in or crowding out of domestic investment by FDI in China in the period up to 1996. However, single country econometric studies are highly questionable as relevant time series are often very short and the danger exists that other exogenous factors are responsible for domestic investment have not been included into the equation. Thus, it might be helpful to consider the theoretical arguments that would support or weaken the argument of crowding out effects on domestic investment by FDI in China.

---

[9] The policy has become most evident in the increase in foreign exchange that Chinese tourists are allowed to take with them when travelling abroad. See: China to give its citizens more freedom in forex purchase, *China Daily*, 4 September 2003.

In principle, the larger the share of FDI going into a sector in a developing country in which there were previously no companies, and the more the FDI is complementary to the horizontal economic structure, the less plausible crowding out appears to be (Agosin and Mayer 2000). A similar argument applies to the vertical relationship of FDI with the host economy. The more complementary the production stage to the host economy, the larger the chance of crowding in, as the FDI might then lead to additional investment in upstream and downstream production. If FDI is in an isolated activity without upstream and downstream links, there might not be much direct crowding out, but there may possibly be indirect crowding out as the FDI might still use the same scarce inputs such as qualified labour.

For the past decade, however, there is little evidence that foreign-owned enterprises have taken away scarce resources from domestic firms in China. Labour, the main local input of foreign affiliates, has been abundant, especially if one assumes that multinational enterprises (MNEs) had to train their own workers and – as they invested in sectors that had not existed before in China – could not hire trained workers from existing firms.

Moreover, as the largest part of foreign direct investment in China from the 1990s onwards has been of efficiency-seeking kind geared at export markets in which China did not play an important role prior to the opening of the economy (and has shown heavy emphasis on the assembly stage), it cannot be argued that foreign firms took sales opportunities from domestic Chinese firms.[10] A large part of the assembly trade can be expected to be conducted by MNEs which treat assembly stage as an integrated part of the production network. An independent domestic firm would not have been able to gain market shares in such assembly business. Another hint that FDI has helped China to gain access to new markets – at least for those provinces that are most important for Chinese exports – is the fact that the causality between FDI and exports is bi-directional (Zhang and Felmingham 2001). This might be a sign that for these provinces, FDI has helped

---

[10] Note that the case might have been slightly different in the textile sector. With textiles losing significant for overall Chinese exports, this is not of much importance for the latest efficiency-seeking foreign direct investments.

to open export markets instead of just taking developing export opportunities from domestic producers.

However, the question remains whether the FDI in assembly industry has brought any additional benefits to the Chinese economy. There is some evidence that FDI helped to integrate China in a regional production chain. Especially since the mid-1990s, labour-intensive exports have lost importance relative to capital-intensive export goods. If we take a look at the development of the Samuelson-RCA indices for Chinese exports over the past decade,[11] the peak for clothing exports, a traditional labour-intensive good, was reached in 1994, and those for toys and other gaming and sporting goods in 1998. At the same time, office machines, telecommunication equipment and other electrical machinery gained in importance (Figure 4 and Table 2). In absolute importance, office machinery has almost caught up with clothing, and in 2002 seven out of the top ten export goods have not been simple products such as footwear or clothing, but more elaborated products such as machinery or appliances. However, most of these goods are – different from textiles – not entirely produced in China, but only some (mostly final) production stages take place there.

For an increasing part of Asian exports to the United States and Europe, China has thus become the final assembly stage (Lemoine and Ünal-Kesenci 2002; Ng and Yeats 2003). Moreover, there are some signs that upstream linkages from assembly trade are building up and the depth of value added in Chinese production is increasing and thus a crowding in might occur. Figure 5 shows the ratio of the import value of inputs of certain components and the final output of finished goods for a few selected items.[12] As can easily be seen, the

---

[11] Of course, Samuelson's revealed comparative advantage (RCA) index does not necessarily tell anything about real comparative advantages, as a country might find itself for historical reasons exporting goods in which it does not really have a comparative advantage, or industrial policy has pushed exports which are not those goods in which a country has a comparative advantage from its initial endowments. However, it is a useful proxy to show in which sectors a country exports a lot.

[12] For colour TVs, the ratio of imports of TV tubes to TV sets produced is plotted; for cars the ratio of car parts to cars produced and for microcomputers the ratio of parts for them to actual units produced.

Figure 4
CHINA'S RCA FOR 5 TOP EXPORT GROUPS IN 2002

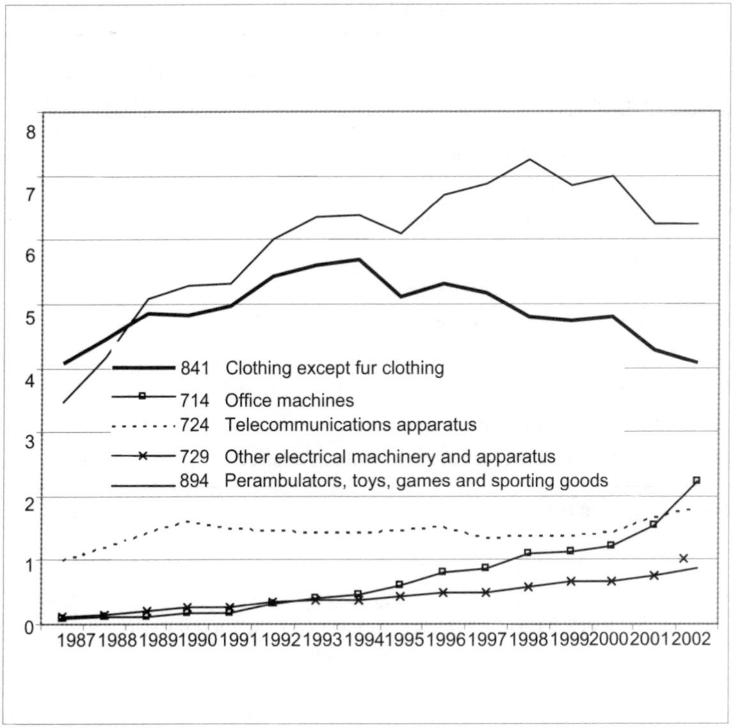

▬▬ 841	Clothing except fur clothing
─□─ 714	Office machines
·······724	Telecommunications apparatus
─×─ 729	Other electrical machinery and apparatus
▬▬ 894	Perambulators, toys, games and sporting goods

Source: Author's calculations based on UN Comtrade database.

ratio of output to imported parts has increased for both TVs and computers, but fallen for cars – cars are not an important export product for China, as they are mainly assembled for sale in the domestic market.

Another indicator for the increase of domestic value added in the assembly industries is the relative depth-of-value-added (RDVA). The indicator shows the ratio of exports in a certain category to imports of parts for a similar SITC category and compares this ratio to the rest of the world. Values above 1 show that this sector generates more value added in foreign trade than other countries, values below 1 show that the value added is comparatively low. As can be seen in Figure 6, the depth of Chinese production of office machinery and data processing equipment (SITC-classification 759)

Table 2
CHINA'S TOP 10 EXPORTS IN 2002
(3-digit SITC codes)

SITC	Description	*Share of China's Exports (In per cent)*
841	Clothing except fur clothing	12.5
714	Office machines	10.7
724	Telecommunications apparatus	6.8
729	Other electrical machinery	4.7
894	Perambulators, toys, games, sporting goods	3.9
891	Musical instruments, sound recorders	3.4
722	Electric power machinery and switch	3.4
851	Footwear	3.3
719	Machinery and appliances-non electrical	2.9
861	Scientific, medical, optical meas./contr. instruments	2.1

Source: UN Comtrade database.

Figure 5
RATIO OUTPUT VOLUME TO VALUE OF IMPORTED PARTS
(1995 = 100)

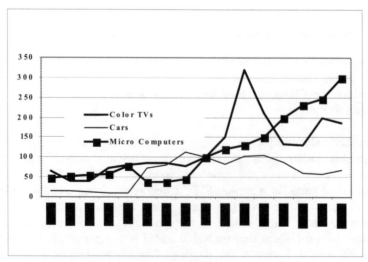

Source: Author's calculations based on UN Comtrade and Chinese Statistical Office data.

Figure 6
RELATIVE VALUE ADDED FOR DIFFERENT PRODUCTS

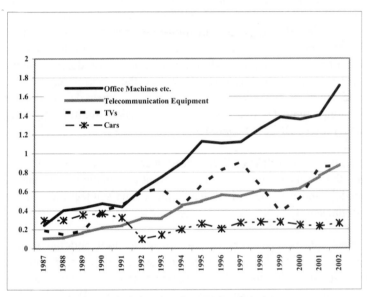

Source: Author's calculations based on UN Comtrade data.

has increased over recent years and now stands at a higher level than the global average. For telecommunication equipment, this indicator has also risen, but has not yet reached the global average. The same is true for TVs even though the upward trend came temporarily to a standstill in 1999/2000.

Finally, there are even some indications of a technology spillover. Case-studies on the micro-level point to positive spillover effects from FDIs (Fan 2003:50). Cheung and Lin (2004) also find evidence that on a provincial level, FDI seems to have a positive impact on patent applications from domestic Chinese firms. Thus, the evidence points toward FDI having, in fact, helped the development of a competitive manufacturing industry, at least in some sectors. Given the large weight of foreign firms in the country's exports, FDI seems to have contributed strongly to China's good export performance over the past decade.

It remains open to debate, however, how quickly China might have integrated into the world economy without FDI. According to Zhang and Felmingham (2001) those provinces with only moderate FDI activity have also experienced impressive export growth, even if it was significantly lower than in high-FDI provinces. In these cases, exports seem to have Granger-caused FDI. This might be seen as an indication that given enough time a competitive domestic export industry would have developed. However, the superior penetration of world markets by foreign companies compared to domestic companies indicates that this would have taken significantly longer than a rather FDI-based approach.

Thus, the large inflow of FDI indeed seems to have helped China to reap the fruits of its favourable currency valuation over the past decade[13] and also helped to accelerate China's integration into the regional supply chain.

A final question is whether the inflow of FDI and the resulting repatriation of profits have burdened the Chinese current account to such an extent that the risk of a currency crisis may have increased. So far, this does not seem to have been the case. As most FDI into China has so far been of the efficiency-seeking kind, i.e. setting up production for export, there should not have been any negative effect on the future outlook of the current account. This kind of FDI has, in fact, helped China penetrate world markets and helped it earn foreign exchange. Even if part of the income earned is transferred abroad, the net effect on the current account is expected to be positive.

In conclusion, the evidence seems to suggest that FDI in China has, so far, had an overall positive effect on the Chinese economy, even though some of the benefits could probably also have been reaped without foreign capital, albeit at a slower pace.

---

[13] For the relevance of the currency valuation on Chinese development, see Dullien (2004b).

III. IMMINENT TRENDS IN CHINESE FDI

Purely resource- and efficiency-seeking FDI has, in recent years, gradually been supplemented, and to a certain extent, been replaced by market-seeking FDI. There are a number of reasons why we can expect this trend to continue over the next few years.

III.1. WTO accession

First, with the country's accession to the World Trade Organization (WTO), China has pledged to grant foreign companies greater access to previously sheltered service sectors such as financial services, insurance, legal services and telecommunications. This may lead to more market-seeking FDI. This is especially true in high-end services, e.g. financial services and insurance. Western governments, including the United States Government, therefore hope that their companies will have a competitive advantage. Moreover, the service sector is by definition a sector in which the product is hard to export as close proximity to the customer is necessary, even though some services become increasingly tradeable because of the technological progress in communication technology.[14] Consequently, implementation of the WTO accession agreement will most likely result in an increase in market-seeking FDI into newly opened sectors.

The effect might be slightly different for those manufacturing sectors which have, in principle, been opened up to foreign investment but in which high import tariffs have provided a strong incentive to companies to operate in China in order to circumvent tariffs. The automobile sector might be a good example of such a development: With tariff rates once standing at 100 per cent, global car companies have invested in China to assemble cars for the domestic market. In principle, the agreed tariff cuts to a maximum of 47 per cent (OECD 2002) will lower incentives to conduct market-seeking investment in these sectors. However, this trend may to a certain extent be compensated for by the desire of manufacturing companies to have subsidiaries in their customers' markets to shield from exchange rate fluctuations. Moreover, the perspective of WTO accession should

---

[14] See for a discussion also UNCTAD (2004b).

have already dampened market-seeking FDI in relevant sectors as the timetable and framework for tariff reduction has been known for some time and firms should have anticipated the impact this may have on the attractiveness of producing in China for the Chinese market. Thus, the gross negative effect of WTO accession on market-seeking FDI in manufacturing should be negligible, rendering the net effect of WTO accession on overall market-seeking FDI strongly positive.

Finally, falling barriers against Chinese products in other WTO member states will make China more attractive as a production platform for further re-export. This might have some positive influence on further efficiency-seeking FDI in the export sector. The effects of the elimination of textiles export quotas at the beginning of 2005, on the other hand, has to a certain extent been counteracted by a new export tax on Chinese textile exports. Thus, as China will be opening up several sectors formerly closed to foreign companies while the fall of further quota and tariff barriers in Chinese export markets will only be incremental, WTO accession is expected to have a much larger impact on market-seeking than on efficiency-seeking FDI.

III.2. Real appreciation

Second, the continuing real appreciation of the renminbi will also alter the amount and composition of FDI. Since the mid-1990s, the real effective exchange rate has been on an upward trend. Measured in unit labour costs, China has appreciated in real terms by roughly 25 per cent vis-à-vis the main trading partners (Dullien 2004b). The real appreciation is mainly due to a slow increase of Chinese unit labour costs since the late 1990s while unit labour costs in other Asian countries have, in fact, fallen after the Asian Crisis. The current strong economic growth and pick-up in measured domestic inflation will most likely intensify this trend as it will exert upward pressure on wages. Given the de facto fixed exchange rate, this would inevitably lead to a real appreciation. Another element which, of course, would lead to a further real appreciation would be any nominal rise in the renminbi, as it has been discussed among academic and private sector economists since late 2003.[15]

No matter whether real appreciation stems from the increase in domestic wages or in a nominal appreciation of the Chinese currency, it would dampen efficiency-seeking FDI. In the event of a real appreciation, producing for export in China would become less profitable as all domestic inputs become more expensive in foreign currency. While the costs for intermediary imports remain unchanged in foreign currency, either profit margin would have to fall or sales prices in export markets would have to increase. Both options would lead to a reduction of profits in the export sector: Falling profit margins would directly dampen profits while an increase in sales prices would indirectly dampen profits by lowering sales volume and thus absolute profits. In this scenario, efficiency-seeking investments would become less attractive.

However, as long as real appreciation does not hinder domestic income creation and is compensated by stronger domestic demand, market-seeking FDI becomes more attractive. First, with real wages rising, the purchasing power of Chinese customers would increase, thus also increasing business opportunities for foreign companies. Second, with a real appreciation, profits in business tailored for the domestic Chinese markets would become larger in dollar terms. This again might make market-seeking FDI in China more attractive.

Thus, the current trend of a real appreciation of the Chinese currency will, without any doubt, lead to a decrease in efficiency-seeking FDI and most likely to an increase in market-seeking FDI.

III.3. Opening of the capital account

The gradual opening of the capital account might also influence the composition and volume of FDI. As the repatriation of profits and reversal of investment undertaken in China has so far been limited, any liberalization of capital account regulations would potentially increase the attractiveness both for market-seeking and efficiency-seeking FDI. However, as the repatriation of earned foreign exchange

---

[15] See exemplarily Williamson (2003) or Greenspan (2003).

in the export sector is already much further liberalized than the repatriation of profits in companies providing for the domestic market,[16] FDI in the latter will gain relatively more attraction. Thus, the opening of the capital account would also let us expect an increase in market-seeking FDI.

Thus, overall, we can safely expect that there will be a shift from the efficiency seeking FDI in the export sector to FDI in sectors providing for domestic markets.

IV. POTENTIAL PROBLEMS

As has been pointed out before, the effects of market-seeking FDI might be quite different from those of efficiency-seeking FDI. In many instances, they compete much more directly with existing firms, especially in developing countries formerly closed to international trade. Moreover, they compete for domestic demand, not for world market demands. These two characteristics might pose problems.

IV.1. Increased crowding out of domestic firms

The first question would be whether market-seeking FDI has, in principle, a higher propensity to crowd out domestic enterprises than efficiency-seeking FDI. For those sectors which have to date been sheltered against foreign competition, this will without any doubt be the case. Possible examples for such a mechanism could include the banking or automobile sectors. In both markets, domestic Chinese firms are widely believed to have technological disadvantages compared with new entrants. These often date back to the legacy of complete state control over the private sector. In banking, for example, domestic financial institutions are burdened with large amounts of non-performing loans.[17] In the medium term, banks will have to write off these loans and incur associated costs. Foreign

---

[16] For details on foreign exchange restrictions, refer to IMF (2004) and previous issues.

[17] Current estimates are that non-performing loans constitute up to 40 per cent of China's annual GDP or slightly less than a third of total outstanding loans. See: Root and Branch, *The Economist*, 4 November 2004.

entrants in the market which are not burdened with these costs would be able to offer higher interest rates on deposits and/or lower rates on loans. Given the large proportion of non-performing loans in the Chinese banks' portfolios, this competitive advantage might be rather large and could lead to a quick erosion of domestic players' market shares.

A similar argument can be made for cars, exemplarily for manufacturing sectors producing for the domestic Chinese market. With as many as 200 independent car producers and many of them only producing a few hundred units a year, the Chinese car industry is very fragmented (Zheng and Hu 2004). This fragmentation is founded on political reasons, some of them going back to the pre-reform area. At that time, the Chinese Government in many sectors promoted provincial autonomy. Moreover, provincial politicians are often judged by growth and employment performance in their region, making them very protective towards regional industries. They will try to keep local firms from going bankrupt, thus hindering consolidation. As most Chinese car firms are too small to efficiently carry out research and development or to reap benefits from learning-by-doing or achieving economies of scale, this prevention of consolidation hurts the competitiveness of domestic firms. Foreign companies entering the market, in contrast, do not face such a problem. Instead, they can even profit from learning-by-doing and achieving economies of scale in the world market. There is even a danger that they may gain market shares very quickly against Chinese producers and push them out of the market. This may be a reason for concern as foreign automobile companies may both carry out research and development as well as produce more complicated and sophisticated car parts in their home countries. Given that research and development as well as the production of technology-intensive car parts have positive external effects on the regional economy, this might mean a slower technological development for China. This problem also seems to have been recognized by Chinese authorities as, by 2010, they want 50 per cent of the cars produced in China to be built by purely Chinese companies that own 100 per cent of the technologies used (cf. *Automotive News*, 9 June 2003).

The question remains, however, whether the negative effects for the Chinese economy will be compensated by enhanced quality and/or lower costs of services and manufacturers in which foreign firms crowd out domestic players. In principle, one could imagine that the fall in prices of a good or service brought about by the increased efficiency of foreign over domestic producers yields sufficient advantages for other sectors which, in turn, gain competitiveness helping them to reap benefits bigger than the adverse effects on economic growth brought about by the initial crowding-out. However, such effects can be primarily expected from goods and services which are used as inputs from other firms. As a large proportion of manufactured goods are in fact consumer goods, a positive growth effect cannot be expected from an efficiency increase in these sectors due to a crowding out of domestic activity. The same is true for those services which are mainly provided for final consumption in the country itself. However, as services tend to have less pronounced upward and downward linkages, a crowding out of service firms producing for domestic consumers might not have as much adverse impact as a crowding out of manufacturers producing for the domestic market. Thus, in principle, a crowding out in the manufacturing sector producing for the domestic market might be the worst kind of crowding out by FDI, followed by a crowding out of services geared for domestic consumers. The most harmless type of crowding out would be in the service sector providing services for other businesses as the positive consequences might offset the negative effects. This argument would also fit nicely with the empirical results from Nunnenkamp and Spatz (2003). According to them, market-seeking FDI in manufacturing has negative effects on the economic growth in the host country, while both efficiency-seeking FDI in manufacturing and market-seeking FDI in the service sector have slightly positive effects.

IV.2. Balance of payment problems

The second question is whether the shift from efficiency-seeking to market-seeking FDI will have any medium- or long-term implications on the balance of payments. In order to answer this question, we have to analyse whether the type and structure of FDI influences the pattern of profit repatriation the foreign owner will decide on. A higher rate of profit repatriation constitutes a higher permanent burden on the current account as repatriated profits appear in the balance of payments as income paid to the rest of the world. This would increase the need for capital inflows in the future as it might tilt the balance of payments' current account into a downward trend or aggravate a future current account deficit.

Since the de facto pegging of the renminbi exchange rate in 1994, Chinese officials have carefully tried to avoid current account deficits. Avoiding becoming reliant on capital inflows to finance domestic consumption and investment must be seen in the context of the emerging market currency crises which occurred in recent decades. In developing countries, foreign capital inflows have proved to be very volatile and susceptible to sudden reversals, forcing economic policy to use its macroeconomic instruments to dampen domestic economic growth so that the current account is adjusted rather than promoting domestic growth and stabilizing output and employment. As the financial market scare in the run-up to the Brazilian election in 2002 has shown, this problem is not only valid in the case of a fixed exchange rate, but might even be a problem for countries with a floating exchange rate. Thus, the only safe strategy for a developing country seems to become independent from capital imports (Dullien, 2003). The Chinese government has pursued this very strategy over recent years and has thus helped the country avoid a crisis in the regional financial turmoil of 1997/1998. In the medium and long term, a higher rate of profit repatriation might endanger this strategy and increase the danger of a future balance of payment or currency crisis.

At first sight, there does not seem to be much difference in the pattern of profit repatriation between efficiency- and market-seeking FDI. Both kinds of investment are arguably undertaken by foreigners to increase their wealth in their home currency. As they can be assumed to mainly consume in their home country, they can be expected to repatriate earnings regardless of whether an investment abroad has been of the efficiency- or the market-seeking kind.[18] However, the two types of investment differ in their net effect on the current account. As long as efficiency-seeking FDI in the export sector is not crowding out domestic companies and can provide an additional source of foreign exchange revenue to a country, this type of FDI has a net positive effect on the current account position. In addition to this, as part of the value-added takes place in the host country and

---

[18] Of course, this is only partly true for the kind of FDI which is only FDI in name, but consists of money funnelled by Chinese residents through Hong Kong or Macao. In these cases, the FDI has no consequence on the overall Chinese current account position

part of it is transformed into local factor incomes, the current account position improves, even if profits are repatriated.

With market-seeking FDI, this situation is fundamentally different: Here, the FDI does not help the host country earn any foreign exchange. Instead, the foreign investment is completely oriented to domestic demand and any profits will be earned from domestic demand. The more successful foreign companies strive to both penetrate and earn profits in the market – the larger are the profits, thus the larger its future repatriation. This trend will be further exacerbated when foreign companies producing for the domestic market use foreign capital goods and foreign intermediary products to a larger extent than domestic firms. In these cases, there is a further autonomous shift towards substituting domestic production by imports, further burdening the current account. In fact, there is a lot of anecdotal evidence that foreign firms bring with them machinery from their traditional home suppliers, hinting that this effect might in fact be quite strong.

A sharp shift from efficiency-seeking FDI to market-seeking FDI would thus add to the trend of a deteriorating China's current account balance. This would – if not counteracted by other macroeconomic or exchange rate policy measures – increase the probability that China will turn to a net capital importer in the not too distant future. This would have the effect of making the country more vulnerable to shifts in investor sentiment and ultimately to a balance-of-payment crisis.

V. POLICY CONCLUSIONS

Thus, with the imminent and already ongoing shift from efficiency-seeking to market-seeking FDI in China, the largest part of macroeconomic benefits to be reaped from foreign investment in China might have already been harvested. Future market-seeking FDI might still bring some efficiency increases in certain sectors, but may well be different from the efficiency-seeking FDI in the export sector which hardly carried any economic costs. The new type of FDI will most likely carry macroeconomic burdens which, in some cases, might even more than offset the potential benefits. The challenge for the years to come will thus be to keep the unwanted consequences of market-seeking FDI under control.

V.1.   Strengthening domestic firms

One central point will be to strengthen domestic firms against foreign competition so that some of them will be able to survive increasing competition with foreign entrants into their market. To this end, it is necessary to treat domestic private firms better than in the past. There are substantial indications that domestic private firms are discriminated in comparison with to foreign-owned firms and state-owned enterprises in legal, tax and regulatory matters (Huang 2003). While there might be a rationale for preferring SOEs over other types of companies as SOEs are burdened with obligations to fulfil various policy goals from supporting social stability by sustaining excess employment to stabilizing aggregate demand with their investments, the fact that foreign-owned firms are treated better than domestically-owned private firms does not have any economic rationale. Reducing the burden on domestically-owned private enterprises might enable them to compete more successfully with foreign firms both in domestic sectors hitherto closed to foreign competition and in export markets.

Another necessity might be to allow a certain consolidation. According to Zheng and Hu (2004) there are 200 independent producers of automobiles in China. Cement is produced in more than 8,000 independent firms compared to 110 in the United States, 58 in Brazil and 106 in India. This high fragmentation keeps firms from reaping the full benefits of economies of scale as well as from learning by doing. Moreover, it can be expected that in sectors with a high degree of R&D such as cars, the over-fragmentation hinders innovation as most producers are too small to invest heavily in R&D. The government should therefore take a less prohibiting stance vis-à-vis consolidation among domestic firms than it has done up to now. As regional governments exert a strong influence on local economics, more pressure from the central government may be needed.

Finally, the access of domestically-owned private firms to the financial system needs to be improved. According to a World Bank survey, access to long-term loans is the most pressing problem for private Chinese firms. In 2003, only 1.2 per cent of total outstanding loans concerned private enterprises and individuals, while the private sector accounted for roughly half of the economy's production. Huang (2001) even argues that a significant share of efficiency-seeking FDI inflows can be explained by the fact that domestic firms had no access to domestic finance and are forced to sell part of their businesses to foreign investors. Reforming the banking system in such a manner as to ensure that it becomes more accommodating towards the private sector would allow privately-owned Chinese firms to grow faster as they would neither be required to earn profits before they invest as is often the case today nor to get foreign finance for their investment.

An alternative to strengthening domestic firms appears to introduce local contents regulation, thereby forcing foreign entrants to use downward linkages. However, such regulations are difficult to enforce and may lead to foreign firms adopting strategies to circumvent regulations.[19] As a strengthening of domestic firms yield additional benefits as distortions are removed, this approach should be seen as a priority.

V.2. Managing the real appreciation

A second important point is that the consequences of the shift in the type of FDI on the current account will need to be monitored when making choices on exchange rate and macroeconomic policies. With FDI becoming more market-seeking, the FDI-induced debit of the current account will increase over the medium term. This will add to the recent trend of a shrinking Chinese current account surplus. Against this background, proposals for an appreciation of the renminbi should be considered with great caution, as they would further strengthen this trend and make China dependent on foreign capital inflows to finance the current account deficit, thereby increasing the danger of a balance of payment crisis in the medium- and long-term future.

In this context, another important question is how much inflation and wage increases can be tolerated before the medium-term sustainability of the current account surplus is endangered. With a de facto fixed-exchange rate any domestic wage increases in excess of wage increases introduced by competitors dampen international competitiveness; they also have the potential to impact negatively on the current account balance – just as certain FDI inflows might in the

---

[19] Chapter IV in UNCTAD (2003) deals with possible incentives and regulations on foreign firms to limit unwanted effects and discusses possible problems.

medium term through the channel of profit repatriation. Thus, the tolerance for excessive wage increases should decrease with an increase in market-seeking FDI. At the same time, keeping wage increases in line with productivity growth plus price increases in the home countries of the most important international competitors may also slow the trend from efficiency-seeking to market-seeking FDI as labour remains comparatively cheaper and the purchasing power (in dollar terms) of consumers remain lower.

As wage setting in China's private domestic firms is hardly regulated and uncoordinated across firms, keeping wage increases under control is crucial in efforts to keep the economy from overheating.[20] To this end, an active fiscal policy should be continued to be used. As the investments of SOEs play a large role in aggregate demand (Dullien 2004a), their actions must also be taken into account in macro-economic demand management. Monetary policy is to a certain extent restrained by the fixed-exchange rate. Given that the capital account is not completely closed, the central bank will have to keep interest rates roughly aligned to United States interest rates. However, the room for manoeuvre that monetary policy still possesses should be used to stop the economy from overheating. Moreover, the Chinese central bank has used its influence over final loan rates and administrative measures to slow credit growth wisely to cool the economy in 1994/1995, and has recently begun to use them for the same purpose. As long as these instruments are still compatible with current efforts to deregulate the financial sector, they should also be used for purposes of macroeconomic stabilization.

---

[20] Such a stabilization policy is supported by the stability-oriented wage-setting in state-owned enterprises. However, with a diminishing weight of SOEs in the economy, an increasing part of the stabilization require-ments will fall on monetary and fiscal policy (Dullien 2004b).

REFERENCES

ADB (2004). Foreign Direct Investment in Developing Asia. In: *Asian Development Outlook 2004*, 213–263. Asian Development Bank, Manila.

Agosin MR and Mayer R (2000). Foreign investment in developing countries. Does it crowd in domestic investment? *UNCTAD Discussion Paper*, No. 146, February. United Nations Conference on Trade and Development, Geneva.

Aitken B and Harrison A (1999). Do domestic firms benefit from direct foreign investment? Evidence from Venezuela. *American Economic Review*, 89:605–618.

Bayoumi T, Coe DT and Helpman E (1999). R&D spillover and global growth. *Journal of International Economics*, 47:399–428.

Carkovic M and Levine R (2002). Does foreign direct investment accelerate economic growth? Available at: http://www.worldbank. org/research/conferences/financial_globalization/fdi.pdf.

Cheung KY and Lin P (2004). Spillover effects of FDI on innovation in China: Evidence from the provincial data. *China Economic Review*, 15:25–44.

De Gregorio J (1992). Economic growth in Latin America. *Journal of Development Economics*, 39:59–84.

Dullien S (2003). Währungsregime in Lateinamerika. Die jüngsten Krisen als Bankrotterklärung der orthodoxen Politikempfehlungen. In: Bodemer D, Nolte D und Sangmeister D, eds., *Lateinamerika Jahrbuch 2003*, Frankfurt.

Dullien S (2004a). Measuring China's fiscal policy stance. Unpublished, available at: http://www.dullien.net/pdfs/chinafiscal.pdf.

Dullien S (2004b). China's changing competitive position: Lessons from a unit-labour-cost-based REER. Unpublished, available at http://www.dullien.net/pdfs/ulcchina.pdf.

Dunning JH (1998). Globalization and the new geography of foreign direct investment. *Oxford Development Studies*, 26:47–70.

Fan EX (2003). Technological spillovers from foreign direct investment – a survey. *Asian Development Review*, 20:34–56. Asian Development Bank, Manila

Greenspan A (2003). Remarks by Chairman Alan Greenspan before the World Affairs Council of Greater Dallas, Texas, 11 December. Available at http://www.federalreserve.gov/boarddocs/speeches/2003/20031211/default.htm.

Huang Y (2001). Why more is actually less: new interpretations of China's labor-intensive FDI. Available at http://eres.bus.umich.edu/docs/workpap-dav/wp375.pdf.

Huang Y (2003). One country, two systems: foreign-invested enterprises and domestic firms in China. *China Economic Review*, 14:404–416.

IMF (2004). *Annual Report on Exchange Arrangements and Exchange Restrictions, 2004*, Washington DC, International Monetary Fund.

Kokko A (1994). Technology, market characteristics, and spillovers. *Journal of Development Economics*, 43:279–293.

Lemoine F and Ünal-Kesenci D (2002). China in the international segmentation of production process. *CEPII Working Paper*, No. 2002-02, Paris.

Ng F and Yeats A (2003). Major trade trends in East Asia. What are their implications for regional cooperation and growth? *World Bank Policy Research Working Paper*, No. 3084. Washington DC, World Bank.

Nunnenkamp P and Spatz J (2003). Foreign direct investment and economic growth in developing countries: how relevant are host-country and industry characteristics? *Kiel Working Paper*, No. 1176, Kiel Institute for World Economics.

OECD (2002). *China in the World Economy: The Domestic Policy Challenges*. Paris, Organisation for Economic Co-operation and Development.

UNCTAD (2003). *World Investment Report 2003: FDI Policies for Development*. United Nations publication, Sales No. E.03.II.D.8., New York and Geneva.

UNCTAD (2004a). Macroeconomic conditions behind China's spectacular growth experience since the mid-1990s. Mimeo.

UNCTAD (2004b). *World Investment Report 2004: The Shift Towards Services*. United Nations publication, Sales No. E.04.II.D.36, New York and Geneva.

Williamson J (2003). The renminbi exchange rate and the global monetary system. Lecture delivered at the Central University of Finance and Economics, Beijing, 29 October.

Wolf C Jr, Yeh KC, Zycher B, Eberstadt N and Sung-Ho Lee (2003). *Fault Lines in China's Economic Terrain*. Santa Monica, CA, Rand Corporation.

Zhang Q and Felmingham B (2001). The relationship between inward direct foreign investment and China's provincial export trade. *China Economic Review*, 12:82–99.

Zheng J and Hu A (2004). An empirical analysis of provincial productivity in China (1979–2001). *Working Paper in Economics (SwoPEc)*, No. 127, ISSN 1403–2465. Available at http://www.handels.gu.se/epc/archive/00003451/01/gunwpe0127rev1.pdf.

MARKET OPENING, ENTERPRISE LEARNING AND INDUSTRY TRANSFORMATION – A CASE STUDY OF CHINA'S CAR INDUSTRY[1]

Hong Song and Chai Yu[2]

Abstract

On the basis of neo-classical and structural researches upon industrial development and market environment, this paper explores the changes of strategic adjustment and relative competition advantage of multinational enterprises and indigenous firms in auto industry after the WTO accession, and forecasts the future development trend of this industry in terms of the ability of learning and adaptation in indigenous firms. The approach of this research is to utilize the analytic framework of interactive learning and industrial development and consider fully the features of industrial expansion in developing countries.

INTRODUCTION

Mainstream western economists criticize developing countries for protecting their infant industries because they maintain it does not help local enterprises to grow but, on the contrary, lead to low efficiency and resource wastages. Even if the enterprises manage to grow, they can hardly withstand the challenges of international competition. To them, developing countries should not protect their infant industries at all. Instead, those countries should totally liberalize their trade and investment regimes.

On the contrary, structurism (or evolutionary economics) holds that the source of economic development of developing economies mainly comes from acquiring and assimilating advanced international management skills, technology and machinery and equipment manufacturing skills by local enterprises and industries instead of simple capital accumulation. Nelson and Pack (1999) call

---

[1] This research is supported by Chinese National Natural Science Foundation and Oxfam (Hong Kong).
[2] The opinions expressed in this paper are those of the authors and do not necessarily reflect the views of UNCTAD. The authors remain solely responsible for any shortcomings in this paper.

those arguments "assimilation theories", and the mainstream one "accumulation theories" (Krugman 1994, 1997, 1998). They have also analysed the impact of multinational enterprises on the learning and innovative abilities of Newly Industrializing Economies (NIEs) (Kim and Nelson 2000). Some young scholars from this school have recently analysed the issue of multinational enterprises and the industrial development of NIEs (Cyhn 2002 and Poon 2002). However, these studies have not taken into account the restrictions placed by the international environment on the capability building within enterprises and the degree and scope of industrial development in developing economies (Fransman 2000:216–225).

Drawn upon the above study on the relations between industrial development and the market environment, this paper argues that the extent and speed of the market opening process of developing countries should match the existing competitive advantage of local enterprises, as well as their adaptability and learning ability. Only by doing so will it be possible for developing countries to maintain a sustainable and healthy development of their industries in the international environment.

For large developing countries, implementing the self-dependent economic development and industrial development models should form the basis of the long-term and healthy development of these countries (Hong Song and Chai Yu 1999). At the heart of self-dependent economic and industrial development is the need to cultivate indigenous firms and enhance their technological, management and product development capabilities. In the course of the self-dependent development of industries in a country, market opening and importing of foreign capital must be in keeping with these capabilities. Only so will it be possible for self-dependent industries to develop healthily. If the market were to open too fast and too profoundly, the adaptability or adjusting capability of local enterprises would be overwhelmed by the strength or competitiveness of multinational enterprises. In this situation local self-dependent industries would suffer and a change could occur whereby the self-dependent model could develop into a dependent development model. At the other end of the scale, if a local market were completely closed, it would not be possible for local industries to go back to a state of self-sufficiency without the assistance of multinational enterprises.

China finally became a WTO member in November 2001 after more than ten years of hard bargaining. As a WTO member, the Chinese Government committed itself to fling its door wide open and liberalize the investment regime. Multinational enterprises and local enterprises have all made dramatic adjustments to their development strategies. Chinese industries and even the whole economy have been subject to stern challenges. This paper tries to analyse this process and its impact, taking the car industry as an example. The structure of the paper is as follows: after the introduction, the paper will give a brief account of the process of the opening of China's auto industry. The paper then analyses how multinational enterprises and local enterprises have adjusted their strategies and compared the strength of multinationals and local enterprises and its impact on the development of China's auto industry. The paper ends with some basic conclusions from the case study.

I. OPENING OF CHINA'S AUTOMOTIVE INDUSTRY

China used to have the tariff plus quota system in its automotive industry. As a result of this, the prices of motor vehicles in China were much higher than world prices and the numbers of cars that could be imported was limited. In Figure 1, the world price is P, P+t is the home auto price under the protection of tariffs, P+t+q is the price under the dual protection of tariffs and quotas and license. Correspondingly, the real import is S2D2. In reality, when consumers buy cars they have to pay VAT and consumption tax so the import amount is less than S2D2, it is in fact S3D3.[3] Even if we do not take into account the price effect of the import licenses and import amount and other non-tariff quotas,[4] the auto price in local market is about 1.25–3.45 times the price paid on world markets.

---

[3] Here, the implying assumption is that China is a "small" country in terms of auto import in the world car market; the tariffs and quotas have a direct impact on the price and transferred that effect completely into the price increase at home. This assumption is correct if we take into account the amount of vehicles imported every year by China over the past decade (not more than 200,000 units, averaging about 50,000 a year).

[4] As deducted by the constant of auto import consolidated tax rate, we calculate the balance of (world price + tariff + VAT (17 per cent) + consumption tax (8, 5 and 3 per cent) as the price effect of import licenses and quotas, the effect is basically around 20 per cent. Source: Calculated by the authors according to the import tariffs of different models of vehicles in 2000.

Figure 1
CHANGES IN CHINA'S AUTOMOTIVE MARKET BETWEEN 2000 AND 2006

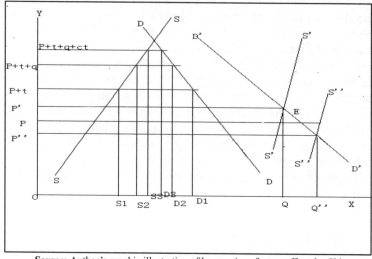

Source: Author's graphic illustration of how various factors affect the Chinese
car market.

Table 1
COMPARISON OF THE AUTO PRICES IN CHINA AND THE WORLD, 1 JANUARY 2000

	Gasoline of over 3.0L, diesel of over 2.5L	Gasoline of under 3.0L, diesel of under 2.5L
Before 1994	3.45P+L+Q	3.45P+L+Q
1 April 1994	2.75P+L+Q	2.35P+L+Q
1 April 1996	2.45P+L+Q	2.25P+L+Q
1 October 1997	2.25P+L+Q	2.05P+L+Q
1 January 2000	2.05P+L+Q	1.95P+L+Q
1 July 2006	1.25P	1.25P

Source: Computation based on data found on website: www.b-car.com.
Note: Computation: Domestic price = International price P + import tariffs +
consumption tax (taken as 8 per cent) +VAT (17 per cent) + L (Licenses) + Q
(Quotas).

Over the past few years, China's opening of its auto market has been accelerated. In 1994–2000 tariffs were reduced by 64–68 per cent from 220 per cent to 70–80 per cent. With China's accession to the WTO, great changes have taken place on China's auto market. First, the major factors influencing auto prices such as import tariffs, VAT (value added tax) and consumption tax have been greatly reduced or scrapped altogether and import licenses and quotas were also abolished. The prices, therefore, dropped significantly, from the current P + t +q +ct down to P' (international price plus 25 per cent tariff); in other words the price falls by 2–5 times of that on the world market down to the level or even lower than the international price (that is, P'' level in the Figure 1).[5] This has the result of bringing the price of cars on the home market into line or on a par with international level. In the two months after November 2001 when China became a WTO member – to 1 January 2002 – tariff for auto import were lowered from 70–80 per cent to 43.8–50.7 per cent, a drop of 36.63–37.42 per cent or 10-15 per cent drop in the ultimate prices.[6]

Second, auto demand grows or rises as per capita income levels and when Government sponsored efforts to encourage car purchases by reducing or even scrapping consumption tax and building roads and parks. The total auto demand curve does not only move outward but also changes in shape, with the demand of low-cost economy cars increasing significantly. There are similarities in auto consumption in the whole world. When a country's per capita income tops US$1,000, it will support a profitable auto industry; when the per capita income reaches US$4,000, cars will enter families on a large scale and stimulate a rapid growth of the local auto industry. In 2003 China's per capita GDP was US$1,000. But as the regional disparities in income are large, in the eastern part of the country per capita GDP reached US$1,400, while it was only US$600 in the western part. The per capita GDP of many large cities in China have reached or approached the auto consumption threshold of US$4,000; for

---

[5] If we take the Renminbi's appreciation trend into account, the drop in China's auto prices would be bigger. The initial estimate is that vehicles priced between RMB50,000–RMB80,000 would become the best selling models.

[6] China became a WTO member on 13 November 2001. In the last two months of 2001 Chinese consumers held onto their savings and waited for China's accession to the WTO. This reflects their concerns on auto prices and on the other hand, they hoped to buy new models of cars.

example in Guangzhou it stands at US$4,568, in Shanghai at US$4,500 and in Beijing at US$3,000.

China is experiencing the fastest economic growth in the world. In 1979–2000, China's GDP grew at an average annual rate of 9.5 per cent and in 2001–2003, growth rate were respectively at 7.3, 7.8 and 9.1 per cent. The plan mapped out by the 16th National Party Congress envisions that growth would quadruple, or grow at an average annual rate of over 7 per cent over the next 20 years. Per capita income levels will rise more quickly to reach US$4000 or even higher, above the threshold for auto consumption. If we take into account the impact of the Renminbi's appreciation, Chinese families will increasingly begin to purchase cars.

Third, the potential for auto development in China is huge. One of the major salient features of China's auto industry is that the market development is fuelled by official purchases. The public vehicle market differs from the private vehicle market which develops according to market demand. The private vehicle market is dominated by cheap and small cars while China's market as a whole is mainly composed of medium- and high-grade cars. Before China's accession to the WTO, there was virtually no development of the private car market.

Fourth, auto supply will increase rapidly as investment restrictions fall, as well as when examination and approval rights are delegated and when performance requirements in terms of local-content, exports, etc, are scrapped. This point also could be surmised from total sales: In 2001, 2002 and 2003, total sales grew by 18.25 per cent (721,463), 56.08 per cent (1,126,029) and 75.09 per cent (1,971,601), respectively.

From 1994 onwards, China's auto industry has undergone extensive and profound reforms and opening up in preparation for joining GATT or WTO, resulting in a big drop in auto prices. In the context of zero or even negative growth in the global car market, China is of great strategic significance to multinational corporations.

Table 2

TARIFF REDUCTION AND WTO COMMITMENTS MADE BY CHINA FOR JOINING GATT OR WTO[1]

Tax Code: motor vehicles for passengers (tax number 87.02 are exceptions) including tourism wagons and racing cars		Spontaneous tariff reduction for joining GATT or WTO					Tariff commitment to WTO concerning auto import							
		Before 1994	1 January 1994	1 April 1996	1 October 1997	1 January 2001	Restrictive tariff at the time of joining WTO	Ultimate restrictive tax rate	Period of implementation	2002	2003	2004	2005	2006
87032130: 1-1.5L (Point ignition engine or gasoline vehicles)		220	110	100	80	70	51.9	25	1 July 2006	43.8	38.2	34.2	30	28/25
87032230	1.5-2.5	220	110	100	80	70	51.9	25	1 July 2006	43.8	38.2	34.2	30	28/25
87032334	2.5-3.0	220	110	100	80	70	51.9	25	1 July 2006	43.8	38.2	34.2	30	28/25
87032430	>3.0	220	150	120	100	80	61.7	25	1 July 2006	50.7	43.0	37.6	30	28/25
87033130: <1.5 (Compression ignition engine or diesel vehicles)		220	110	100	80	70	51.9	25	1 July 2006	43.8	38.2	34.2	30	28/25
87033230	1.5-2.5	220	110	100	80	70	51.9	25	1 July 2006	43.8	38.2	34.2	30	28/25
87033330	>.2.5	220	150	120	100	80	61.7	25	1 July 2006	50.7	43.0	37.6	30	28/25

Source: Compilation of the *Legal Instruments on China's Accession to the World Trade Organization* (WTO 2001).

[1] In part.

II. STRATEGIES OF MULTINATIONAL ENTERPRISES
AND THEIR IMPACT ON CHINA

China's auto industry was mainly dominated by Sino-foreign joint ventures before China became a WTO member (Table 3). In 2000, there were 13 car makers, eight of which were Sino-foreign joint ventures and five were domestic automakers (FAW Red Flag, Tianjin Xiali and three Alto assembly plants). They produced 12 brands, of which 10 were foreign and two were domestic. The market share of Sino-foreign joint ventures was over 85 per cent.

Under tariff and non-tariff protection measures, the investment by multinational enterprises was typically market-oriented, that is to bypass high import barriers to engage in production and operational activities oriented toward the local markets. The products had already been rejected by developed countries and their technical levels and production equipment were far behind advanced world levels and models remained unchanged for scores of years. However, because of protection and lack of competition, these enterprises occupied a monopolistic position on local markets. Although production reached the requirements of the economy of scale, product prices were still far higher than comparable prices on the international market. In 2000 China exported 523 cars, imported 21,620 units, produced 605,000 cars and sold 617,000 cars, as can be seen exports only accounted for 0.086 per cent of production. With regard to production, Shanghai Santana and FAW Jetta both reached the 100,000 units mark, but their price were 4–5 times those found on international markets. The international market price of the Jetta model was around US$5,000, but the price of the same car in China in 2000 was as high as RMB160,000, 4–5 times the international price. In 2000, the main-stream model in China was Shanghai Volkswagen's Santana model. This model had originally been launched on international markets in 1971, but in China the same model was produced in 1985. Jetta was the 1985 international model but in China it was launched in 1992. Fukang was the 1991 model internationally but in China it was brought into circulation in 1996; Alto was the 1984 international model but in China it was introduced in 1991. Xiali was 1980 model but in China it was launched in 1986. What is unimaginable is that 30 year-old Santana model accounted for 30.88 per cent of market share in China in 2000.

After China's WTO accession, changes in demand and supply on the auto market led to multinational enterprises making major changes to their investment strategies.

First, market-oriented investments require big adjustments. Multinational enterprises could either gradually withdraw their investment from China and supply China's market by export, or update the existing production base in China by expanding investment, upgrading technologies and equipment and renewing or increasing new products, and so on. In reality, it turns out to be that the multinationals opted for the latter for the following reasons: (1) Although China has committed to lower tariffs, it would take several years to achieve them and import barriers for auto imports would remain high during the period. This situation will pose great difficulties for multinational to implement their export strategy. The result of this is that it is not feasible to export cars to China. (2) Existing foreign direct investment before China's WTO accession is mainly conducted by European and North American multinationals whose production bases remain in their home countries. It is not viable for these enterprises to export vehicles to China from their local territory or from their production bases overseas. (3) The scale and strategic significance of China's market means that exporting cars to China from other areas does not pay off. So, the German Volkswagen enhanced its joint ventures with the FAW and Shanghai Automotive Industry Corp. Group and upgraded their products. On 15 July 2003, Volkswagen announced that it would invest €6 billion in China over the five-year period between 2003–2007 in order to double the production capacity in Changchun and Shanghai and use 60 per cent of this investment to develop and launch new products. Citroen of France also upgraded its cooperation with the Dongfeng Auto Group and an additional investment of RMB1 billion was made in the joint venture Dongfeng Citroen to raise the registered capital of the joint venture up to RMB7 billion. Shenlong Auto is divided in three parts: one is the manufacturing center; the industrial business department (including R&D center); and two marketing centers to commercialize Peugeot and Citroen cars. Following the import of the ZX series common production platform by Shenlong, the joint venture will import another entirely new common production platform. The two platforms will produce both Citroen and Peugeot, with new models to be produced every year. In 2004, the joint venture launched six new models to expand production capacity from the current 50,000–60,000 units to more

Table 3
CHINA'S MAJOR CAR MAKERS IN 2000

Joint venture	Multinationals	Local enterprises	Effective date of contract	Date of production launch	Registered capital (US$ million)
FAW Volkswagen	Volkswagen	FAW	1990 / 11	1991 / 09	53571
Shanghai Volkswagen	Volkswagen	Shanghai Automotive Corp.	1985 / 02	1985 / 09	8889
Shanghai GM	GM	Shanghai Automotive Industry Corp.	1997 / 04	1998 / 12	70000
Shenlong Co.	Citroen	Dongfeng Auto Corp.	1992 / 04	1992 / 05	61643
Beijing Jeep	Chrysler Co.	Beijing Automotive Group	1983 / 06	1984 / 01	14682
Guangzhou Honda	Honda Co.	Guangzhou Auto Industry (Group) Co.	1997 / 11	1998 / 07	
Guizhou Sukaru	Fuji Heavy Industries		1996 / 07		RMB 300 million
Changan Group	Suzuki Co.	Changan group	1993 / 05	1995 / 05	7000
Xi'an Qinchuan	Suzuki Co.	Xi'an Qinchuan	Non-joint venture		
Jiangnan Auto Industry Co. Ltd.			Non-joint venture		
Jilin Jiangbei Machinery Plant			Non-joint venture		
Tianjin Xiali	Charade Co.	Tianjin Automotive Industry Co.	Non-joint venture		
FAW Co. Ltd.			Non-joint venture		

Source: The Association of Chinese Auto Industry.

Table 3
CHINA'S MAJOR CAR MAKERS IN 2000

Equity ratio	Terms of cooperation	Main brand model	Output in 2000	Sales in 2000	Percentage in domestic output	Percentage in domestic sales (not including imports)
40 : 60	25	Jetta, Audi, Bora	110005	111269	18.18	18.03
50 : 50	25	Santana, Passat, Polo	221524	222432	36.62	36.05
50 : 50	30	Buick, Sail	30024	30543	4.96	4.95
26.875 : 73.125	35	Citroen, Picasso, Elysee	53900	52036	8.91	8.43
42.4 : 57.6	20	Cherokee, Challenger SUV	4867	4628	0.80	0.75
50 : 50	30	Accord, Odyssey	32228	32233	5.33	5.22
25 : 75		Sukaru	855	1470	0.14	0.24
49 : 51	30	Alto, Gazelle	48235	47001	7.97	7.62
		(Assembly) Alto, Flyer	5380	5227	0.89	0.85
		Assembling Alto	343	379	0.06	0.06
		Assembling Alto	0	146	0.00	0.02
		Xiali, Xiali 2000	81951	84951	13.55	13.77
		Red Flag	15365	15345	2.54	2.49
			605000	**617000**	**100**	**100**

than 150,000 units, with the ultimate goal of advancing toward more than 300,000 units annually. Daimler Chrysler has a similar strategy.

There is yet another category of enterprises which, very early on, began to implement their investment strategy with a vision of WTO aceession. GM of the United States and Honda of Japan are examples of such enterprises. In the joint venture project between GM and SAIC, agreed upon in 1997 but officially launched in 1998, GM controlled 50 per cent of the shares by providing the terms and conditions that other multinationals are reluctant to provide. The terms and conditions of this agreement was that GM would transfer its parts technology to the new joint venture, invest US$40 million to set up five technical training centers, and relocate some of the Buick designing work in China. Due to the reluctance of Volkswagen to transfer more parts and components production to China, the relationship between Volkswagen and SAIC experienced some strains and stresses in the process of establishing joint venture. Chrysler Co. was unsuccessful in its bid to produce multifunctional vehicles in Zhanjiang City, Guangdong Province. The more cautious Toyota also lost an opportunity to set up a joint venture with SAIC due to its unwillingness to pay the price.

Second, multinational enterprises from Japan and the Republic of Korea have long tried to export products to China and have, consequently not been very active in investing in the country.[7] Their strategic choice is beyond reproach. (1) Japan and the Republic of Korea are closer to China and it pays off to export their cars to China from their home base. (2) After China's accession to the WTO, China lowered tariffs and non-tariff levels, thereby providing favourable export conditions to these countries. But, their strategy has met stern challenges from multinationals from Europe and the United States, as these companies have gained great market shares and profits by investing in China to supply the local market from their local production plants, and after China's accession to the WTO, they are updating their local production. After a number of years of watching and waiting, Japanese and the Republic of Korea multinationals such as Toyota, Renault-Nissan and Hyundai began to become more active and made their presence increasingly felt. These latecomers

---

[7] Strange enough, United States Ford has also adopted this strategy and did not start its joint venture with Chongqing Chanan until 2001. But the joint venture is rather small, with an investment of less than US$100 million.

introduced their entire series and models to China and planned to make a large-scale investment to bring their production scale up to about 300,000–500,000 units in the next five years. Obviously, investing in China has become a leading strategy of multinational enterprises after China became a WTO member.

Third, there are also differences in strategy between new and old multinational enterprises. In a rapidly growing market, multinationals that have just entered into it are seeking to clinch more new market shares by introducing new products and lowering prices and snatching away market shares of the main players. The competition between old and new multinationals on China's auto market is a typical case in this regard. In 2000, German Volkswagen occupied 53.57 per cent of China's auto market. But three years later, the market share dropped to 35.20 per cent.[8] In 2002, there were more than 200 car models representing 40 brands, with new models accounting for 60 per cent[9] of market share. Many models have been brought into China in the form of CKD (complete knock down) or SKD (semi knock down).

The basic strategy of multinational enterprises after China's accession to the WTO is to invest or expand their investments in China, and continually bring out new products and even introduce whole series of products to China, as well as lower prices.

III. STRATEGIC ADJUSTMENT OF CHINESE AUTOMAKERS

China's domestic enterprises began to change after its WTO accession. Some medium and small enterprises, such as Chery, Geely, Hafei and Huachen, etc., began to elbow into this industry by way of technical cooperation and joint technical development arrangements. At the same time, new joint ventures were also created on a regular basis, for example Beijing Hyundai, Changan Ford and Tianqi-FAW Toyota. In the face of changing market pattern after China's accession to the WTO, there are two dramatically opposite strategic options for

---

[8] This proportion does not account for the impact of imports and exports on market shares and has only been calculated according to the total sales of various automakers. So it overestimated the market shares of Volkswagen in 2002.

[9] China Association of Auto Manufacturers (2003): Economic Operation of the Auto Industry in 2002 and Development Analysis for 2003, p. 8, January.

Chinese automakers. The first one is to enter into joint ventures with as many multinationals as possible with the longest possible cooperation terms, thus forming a pattern of "multilateral tie-up" among local major auto groups and multinationals. The second is to develop independently through joint development and technology imports. Mainstream local carmakers have chosen the first strategy, whereas new and small carmakers have chosen the second one.

Table 4
CHINA'S AUTOMOBILE INDUSTRY: ENTERPRISES AND PRODUCTION

Rank	Enterprises	Production	Share
7	Tianjin Xiali (belonging to FAW)	95 466	4.73
8	Chery (belonging to SAIC)	91 223	4.52
9	Geely Group	71 555	3.54
15	FAW	48 092	2.38
17	Hafei	32 387	1.60
18	Huachen	27 054	1.34
	Sub-total for domestic enterprises	*365 777*	*18.12*
1	Shanghai Volkswagen	405 252	20.07
2	FAW Volkswagen	302 200	14.97
3	Shanghai GM	206 964	10.25
4	Guangzhou Honda	117 178	5.80
5	Shenlong	105 475	5.22
6	Changan Suzuki	102 083	5.06
10	Guangzhou Nissan	66 139	3.28
11	Hainan Mazda (FAW)	54 824	2.72
12	Beijing Hyundai	54 348	2.69
13	Dongfeng Yueda-KIA	52 017	2.58
14	Tianqi-FAW Toyota	49 534	2.45
16	Nanjin Nanya	37 034	1.83
19	Beijing Jeep	19 441	0.96
20	Changan Ford	18 535	0.92
21	Others	62 074	3.07
	Sub-total for joint venture	*1 653 098*	*81.88*
	Total	**2 018 875**	**100**

Source: China Automobile Industry: *Production and Sale News*, January 2004.

Why have large Chinese auto groups opted for such a strategy instead of independent investment expansion? Not only do domestic firms lack this ability, but also they are reluctant to do so. Under high protection, joint ventures could enjoy high profits.

According to FAW's Chief Executive Officer, China's largest motor vehicle producer and the second largest carmaker, the main reason for adopting a joint venture strategy is shortage of funds, outdated technology[10] and an inability to expand on its own. The reason for adopting a joint venture strategy rather than a joint development approach is that FAW's production scale is too small in comparison with the world leading carmakers as its annual output is only 120,000 units. FAW cannot invest in product development as it does not have the same level of resources as multinational carmakers with their capital accumulation of millions of vehicles. In the context of economic globalization, it is possible to follow one's own path when there is a production capacity of several million vehicles. Even with such strengths, it is still necessary to establish joint ventures with foreign companies and participate in the international division of labour and cooperation. FAW's production of trucks ranks third or fourth in the world, but it has no independent product development capacity and technological innovation. This is also reflected in the acquisitions made and expansion undertaken by FAW and SAIC in the past few years. Most of the enterprises acquired by FAW are still products of its joint ventures partners. The only independent brand is Red Flag which does not sell well. The enterprises acquired by SAIC, for example GM Wuling and GM Huayao, all produce GM products.

During our survey, we often asked how long domestic enterprises would fare in joint ventures. Multinationals cooperate in the production of current model, but what about future follow-up models? When will the reliance on multinationals end? FAW's CEO believes that the nature of future technology developments is still hard to determine and that the path leading to the next technological stage has yet to be found. Many other companies are reluctant to deal with these problems. However, from the terms of cooperation of new joint ventures between mainstream local automakers and multinationals, we can gather that they hope to remain tied to multinationals forever. Even when the term of cooperation of 25–30 years has yet to elapse, domestic automakers have been seen to be anxiously seeking to extend the term of continued cooperation. Of course, there are also some automakers that have begun to think about this problem seriously and have begun to undertake some development and technology upgrading. But, is such capacity build-

---

[10] Interview with FAW CEO by Economic Daily reporter Cheng Yuan, May 2000.

ing matched with the process of presumed market opening? Can Chinese enterprises rely on the capacities needed to confront and compete with multinationals? What do Chinese enterprises have to learn from such institutional arrangement of establishing joint ventures in the name of "using market to exchange for technology"? What will they learn in the future? Nobody has yet taken the trouble to think seriously about such problems. Unfortunately, these problems are those that will determine the orientation of the future development of China's automotive industry.

Enterprises engaged in independent development are mainly new or small enterprises that have elbowed their way into the auto industry. The reason they have chosen to take the path of independent development of technology and products is that the Government has not allowed them to have access to the auto industry nor set up joint ventures. However, they are attracted by the high profits of the industry and determined to move in and are hence obliged to follow the independent development path. During interviews, CEOs of many independent development enterprises were frank when they said that were they allowed in the past to enter into joint ventures, they would have been willing, and still are ready to do so in the future. They are now still at the stage of learning and growing. Among them, Chery, Hafei and Geely have basically completed the stage and they have now got the benefit of independent development, that is, being able to control brand and technology and the run of the market. Their profits have also grown.

We have also discovered during the interviews that although those enterprises engaged in independent development of products and technology all have the burning desire to enter into joint ventures with multinationals, they do not rule out the opportunities of developing their own brands and are looking forward to them. But they clearly expressed that it would not do to make them give up their brands and independent development ambitions. Joint venture cooperation can only strengthen their capabilities in this regard but not otherwise.

So, in the general environment after China had become a WTO member, Chinese auto makers have all opted for the strategy of entering into joint ventures or importing new models. Even if the enterprises start independent development and have their own brands, they are still ready to enter into joint ventures with multinationals. It is, therefore, a basic strategic option of Chinese automakers to seek to set up joint ventures and import new models and rely on multinational enterprises.

IV. MARKET OPENING AND THE TRANSITION OF DEVELOPMENT MODEL OF CHINESE CAR INDUSTRY

China's car industry has experienced three stages of development: (1) self-sufficiency; (2) joint venture stage since the beginning of the 1980s; and (3) industry development after WTO accession. The first two stages would give us a background for the last stage which should be the focus of our analysis.

(1) Self-sufficiency stage (before the 1980s)

In the self-sufficiency stage (from the founding of new China in 1949 to the 1980s), the technical and production capabilities of local firms were developed by reverse engineering. Cars were mainly produced by copying existing models as no ties existed between Chinese and foreign enterprises whose products were imitated. China manufactured its Hongqi sedan in this way. In the early 1980s, the domestic auto industry was basically at the development stage of manual and workshop production. In 1980, China produced 5,418 cars and imported 19,570 cars. During this period, exchanges between domestic and foreign enterprises were unidirectional and closed. The domestic car industry failed to overcome the many technological bottlenecks, especially in core technologies.

(2) Before WTO accession

As China adopted its reform and opening up policy, its car industry entered a new development phase by attempting to introduce advanced technologies. However, developed countries, especially Japan, were not interested in China's efforts to introduce new technology. Therefore, from the beginning, the Government had to resort to high tariffs and non-tariff protection measures and develop the industry by establishing joint ventures. During this period, China actually learned in two ways. The first consisted of a strategy featuring a high-starting point, large-scale operations and specialization, examples of this include the Number One Automobile Corporation, based in Changchun, Jilin Province, and the Second

Automobile Corporation, based in Shiyan, Hubei Province. The second strategy consisted of small-scale but fast and accumulative development, as followed by Volkswagen in Shanghai and Honda in Guangzhou. Seen from the actual development result of China's joint ventures, the mode of "small-scale, fast and accumulative development" is more efficient. Apart from the inherent advantages of lesser investment and lower costs, a more important reason is that this development mode is more conducive to improved coordination between multinationals, domestic automakers and parts manufacturers and leads to capacity upgrading. This is manifested in the enhanced localization ratio (Lu 1999).

The interactive learning relationship was established on this basis and it, in turn, pushed forward technological and product upgrading of local components and parts producers. However, the production capacity of the Chinese side in the joint venture automakers did not improve a great deal, particularly in the areas of product development, technological innovation and brand marketing.

(3)   The transformation of the auto industry after WTO accession – dependent development

Regardless of whether or not domestic enterprises have the ability to compete with multinationals within China, market opening and strategic adjustment of multinationals and domestic enterprises is bound to take place. First, domestic firms may have more competitive advantages. Second, if they do not have any competitive advantages, these firms must have the potential to catch up with multinationals in the future.

From the perspective of multinationals, after China's WTO accession, there are two principal constraints blocking their development in China: (1) Multinationals must operate in joint ventures and their equity proportion is not allowed to exceed 50 per cent; and (2) A multinational corporation can only establish two joint ventures in China. In spite of these restrictions, the competitiveness of domestic enterprises at the present time still appears to be weak when compared with multinationals.

Firstly, when compared with Chinese enterprises, multinationals enjoy early-mover advantages as reflected in their brands and models, technologies and management. Few possibilities exist for Chinese enterprises to compete with them. Main local enterprises still hope to rely on joint venture to survive and grow up. Although late-coming small enterprises have been engaged in independent product development, their capabilities are far from mature. These enterprises only entered the car industry in recent years and many of them have not completed the development process of two models (4–5 years).

Secondly, in terms of price, the reduction of tariffs and abolition of non-tariff measures after China's WTO accession have led to a sharp fall in the prices of Chinese auto products. This has been exacerbated by the market competition resulting from the entry of more multinationals. As for the multinational partners of joint ventures, their sale in China's market only accounts for a small part of their global sales, so, the price drop in Chinese car market would have little influence on their global performance.[11] But for the Chinese partner in joint venture, market share in China is all they have, so any changes in price will have a strong impact on them. With a decrease in profits, the potential for accumulating capital for future development will be reduced. Therefore, Chinese partners have to depend heavily on joint ventures and the gap between Chinese partners and multinationals will continue to expand on a steady basis. The challenge of price competition is smaller on those enterprises engaged in independent development. They have a measure of autonomy in production and operations and they do not have to pay large fees for the use of technology, brands and patents. So they enjoy price advantages.

Thirdly, in terms of technology, China would lose the possibility of developing car models based on the local market. Multinational enterprises still follow their unique technological development lines according to the requirements of the market and development of their home countries. For instance, European enterprises produce the most differentiated and highest quality cars by manufacturing in line with the characteristics of the European market; United States automakers mass produce cars thereby making them affordable to all; Japan produces energy-efficient small models because of the constraints posed by energy shortages in Japan. China's market is similar to that

---

[11] If we take the example of Volkswagen, we can find that it occupies the largest proportion of market share in China. In 2002, its auto sales in China alone accounted for 18.12 per cent of its total international sales and its market share in China was only 38.5 percent.

of the United States in terms of size and it is also similar to that of Japan in terms of population density, with limited energy supply. Can Chinese carmakers and the auto industry develop unique advantages in line with the environment and characteristics of the Chinese market? Technically, since Chinese enterprises rely almost entirely on importing or purchasing technology, they have little technical innovation and can only follow their counterparts from developed countries.

Can Chinese enterprises build up advantages after the WTO accession? With regard to the potential of Chinese enterprises to catch up with multinationals in terms of technology, especially for those enterprises engaged in independent product development, it is not easy at all. The cultivation of the independent product development capabilities should go through at least two complete product development processes (4–5 years). The biggest risk in product development is that the investment cannot be recalled. If the market opens, home demand for cars may be satisfied with local production by joint ventures plus imports. Obviously, the risk of developing new products by squeezing the market share of multinational enterprises is much higher. The development cost of a single new model is about US$100 million. If the developed product is not accepted by the market, it would result in bankruptcy for Chinese enterprises. But a large multinational can bear the cost of developing two or three or even more new models. Therefore, the number of Chinese enterprises that could survive and mature in such highly competitive environment would be extremely limited.

Similarly, we could also perhaps ask why China's major joint ventures do not engage in independent product development in the same way as those small local enterprises that have just gained access to the industry. One point of view is that the production scale in major joint ventures is still too small. Another answer from small independent enterprises is quite enlightening. They believe that major Chinese car makers cannot learn how to develop products when entering into joint ventures, nor can they obtain technology. This is determined by the property rights allocation pattern of Sino-foreign joint ventures. In a joint venture, multinational enterprises control technology, the brand, collect royalties, have pricing right, and control the parts and components procurement network, while the Chinese partner has to pay a high-technology user fee, even though the model is not designed for the Chinese market. Second, a joint venture is only concerned with the manufacturing process of a product, not the R&D. For a joint venture, the foreign partner provides the production system and takes the responsibility of troubleshooting. But Chinese partners do not have the opportunity to become involved in, and to learn from, the whole product development and technological innovation process as other links are conducted outside the joint ventures.

The relationship between interactive learning and industrial growth and the relative competitive edge of local enterprises compared with multinationals are core factors determining the industrial growth patterns of developing countries. Seen from the perspective of the dynamic process of industrial growth, the establishment of the interactive learning relationship between local enterprises and multinationals are of crucial importance. As industries in developing countries and regions start to focus on industrial development, the establishment of the interactive learning relationship is, by nature, a process in which local enterprises, under the protection of local governments, absorb advanced foreign technologies, management know-how and production development capacity, as well as introduce innovations based on their own unique local market and resources environment. Therefore, what needs to be emphasized here is that institutional arrangements are of vital importance to the establishment of an interactive learning relationship between local enterprises and multinationals. However, an indisputable fact is that the Chinese Government has been too lenient with domestic partners in joint ventures as they have not set requirements or targets for those Chinese enterprises in terms of technology, product and market, let alone supervise or encourage those enterprises. The result is that joint ventures mainly depend on the brand and technological advantages of foreign companies to make profit in the market while those domestic enterprises that seriously introduce technologies and make innovations to improve production are at a disadvantaged position, resulting in the phenomenon that domestic enterprises compete fiercely to establish joint ventures with foreign companies.

To sum up, seen from the perspective of the strategic adjustments of multinationals and domestic enterprises after China's WTO accession, changes in their relative competitive edges and the fostering of their learning and adapting to new circumstances, dependence of local enterprises on multinationals has deepened.

V. STRATEGIC COUNTERFACTUAL ANALYSIS FOR INDUSTRY TRANSFORMATION

In this section, we will explore the consequences of industry transformation by means of strategic counterfactual analysis. Our survey showed convincing evidence that if multinational enterprises are nowadays partly replacing domestic firms, they could also substitute domestic firms completely without facing any policy restraint. Two further trends have also been gradually emerging. The first is that multinational enterprises are trying to sweep policy constraints aside and draw themselves closer to wholly-owned enterprises. The second is that these corporations are also trying to set up more producing plants to get around the constraints of two joint venture projects ceiling for each MNE. As was mentioned earlier in this paper there is a clause in the regulation of China which states that no MNE can have more than two enterprises. Finally, by controlling brands, technology, product development and patents, MNEs are gradually crowding out domestic firms and building up a monopoly or oligopoly in the domestic market.

What are the consequences of these developments? One has been an intra-industry impact. Domestic firms are being replaced by multinational enterprises. Joint ventures could take the place of domestic firms, as occurred in the case of Tianjin XiaLi with the result that the equity ratio of domestic firms is reduced. Another consequence is that they have an impact on employment and local resources allocation.

Profit losses

After joint ventures become wholly-owned enterprises, a Chinese partner in joint ventures can no longer enjoy the segment of profits which joint ventures could benefit from because of capital drawback. This could be as much as 97,348*62.47 per cent = RMB608.13 billion (in 1990 prices).[12]

---

[12] According to the equity ratio of six joint ventures, we divide total amount of profits and tax (RMB183,042 billion) and get the number of RMB97,348 billion, equivalent to 97,348/183,042 = 53.18 per cent. Here, we do not consider profits shared by Chinese partners in other joint ventures.

Another reason why profits shared by domestic firms could be partly lost is due to the substitution by multinational enterprises. With regard to two domestic firms, we would lose 19,134*55.62 per cent = RMB10,642 billion. The substitution of multinational enterprises could raise the present domestic profit level, resulting in further profit loss. Based upon the ratio of profit and tax to industrial capital, we estimate the loss as following: (1) If domestic industrial capital is used according to multinational enterprises' ratio of profit and tax, the profit and tax should be 29.52 per cent*137,054 = RMB40,455 billion. (2) Except for a RMB19,134 billion which has been created by domestic firms, there is a remaining RMB21,321 billion, which is equal to a net profit of 21,321*55.62 per cent = RMB11,858 billion.

Unemployment increased

After transition from joint ventures to wholly owned enterprises, Chinese senior managers in joint ventures would be replaced by foreigners. This substitution would mean that job opportunities for the Chinese would be greatly reduced. As a result, employment per capital in domestic firms is higher than that in joint ventures. The forecast is that from the total capital of domestic firms, by the end of 2003 the loss would be 13,705,400*(1/103.23–1/245.72) = 76,991 per year·per person (Table 5). If other domestic firms such as Hafei, Geely and FAW, etc. are taken into account, the loss should be greater.

Local resources utilization reduced

The import ratio of multinational enterprises is higher than domestic firms. In 2002, based upon the Top 500 export and import enterprises, net imports by the top five joint ventures amounted to US$2.7 billion which is equivalent to about RMB22.4 billion. In these joint ventures, net imports accounted for 20 per cent of gross industrial output value (Table 6). Estimated from this ratio, after the substitution, just in terms of gross industrial output value from Chery and Geely, net imports would increase by (4.11055+4.3886)*20.32 per cent = RMB1,727 billion, which is about US$0.209 billion. By the end of 2003, the total imports of five joint ventures stood at about 2.7*11 (average production year of joint ventures) = US$29.7 billion. After the substitution, by the end of 2003, the stock of increased net imports could be about US$2.3 billion.

Table 5
IMPACT ON EMPLOYMENT

		2002	2001	2000	1999	1998	Total
Shanghai	(1)	3575	3240	3011	2075		11901
GM	(2)	1603705	1114561	1278294	674698		4671259
Shanghai	(1)	10957	10317	10449	10654	8036	50413
Volkswagen	(2)	3326703	2802116	2049882	1834628	1925634	11938962
FAW	(1)	6563	6112	6056	4880	4078	27689
Volkswagen	(2)	1358932	1102 690	1264361	1222492	1220583	6169057
Guangzhou	(1)	2365	2290	1947	1370	1368	9340
Honda	(2)	408634	311862	227085	119742	75891	1143213
Chongqin	(1)	1362	1228	1187	1104	810	5691
Changan	(2)	165986	149656	71176	39259	23539	449615.6
Shenlong	(1)		5133	5248	4787	5541	20709
Fukang	(2)		1766094	1677053	1636596	1445361	6525104
Shanghai	(1)	4151	3176	681			8008
Cherry	(2)	376682	246841	164360			787883.1
Tianjin	(1)		6603	6902	7950		21455
Xiali	(2)		787759	782409	742384		2312551
Total joint ventures		Average Employment	125743	Total Industrial	30897210	Industrial capital per	245.72
Total domestic firms		Per year	29463	capital	300434	person	103.23

Source: China Auto, various issues.
Notes: (1) Number of employees. (2) Total capital (in RMB10,000s.).

Therefore, under market opening, the substitution of multinational enterprises for domestic firms would result in profit losses, reduced employment and the lowered rate of resources utilization. However, from another angle, if domestic firms were to accelerate the learning process and gradually replace multinational enterprises, the benefits would be remarkable.

Table 6
EXPORT AND IMPORT OF JOINT VENTURES IN 2002
(US$10,000; US$1 = RMB8.27)

	Total imports and exports	Exports	Imports	Net import to gross industrial output value (Per cent)
Shanghai Volkswagen	91948	21	91927	21.26
FAW Volkswagen	101557	2451	99106	27.23
Shanghai GM	40893	1406	39487	16.55
Guangzhou Honda	30668	49	30619	18.41
Shenlong Fukang	15064	817	14247	9.06
Total	280130	4744	275386	20.32

Source: The Association of Chinese Auto Industry.

From the above analysis, we know that independent product development capacities could mature within two complete product development cycles, each one lasting between 24 and 28 months. This means that it will take at least 4–5 years to learn to develop a new product independently. After WTO accession, new enterprises entering this industry will reach this stage in 2005 and 2006.

Table 7 shows that if we assume continued growth over the next 5–10 years, multinational enterprises will continue to grow at the same average pace as in the past,[13] the auto industry in China is expected to continue to expand at two different speeds in the future and the cost of delaying capacity building will be high.

To narrow the distance between domestic firms and multinational enterprises will be a difficult process. Hard learning and capacity building will be needed.

---

[13] Considering that by the end of 2003 transnational corporations get their investment back and the price could be lower in recent years, we think this assumption is appropriate.

Table 7
THE BENEFITS OF LEARNING ON DOMESTIC ENTERPRISES

Year	Total profit and tax		Losses under different learning speed	
	Plan I *If production expands at the speed of 1993-2001*	Plan II *If production expands at the speed of 2001-2003*	Plan I	Plan II
			RMB0.1 billion	RMB0.1 billion
2003	404.81	404.81	5 years after the WTO accession Profit and tax: 1601.88 Profit: 1000.69 Among which enterprises[1]: 468	5 Years after the WTO accession Profit and tax: 3794.23 Profit: 2370.26 Among which enterprises: 1110
2007	695.78	3302.14		
2008	796.67	5580.62		
2009	912.18	9431.24	10 years after the WTO accession Profit and tax: 4 644.97 Profit: 2901.71 Among which enterprises: 1358.58	10 years after the WTO accession Profit and tax: 61189.37 Profit: 38225.00 Among which enterprises: 17896.95
2010	1044.45	15938.80		
2011	1195.89	26936.57		
	The rate of production growth between 1993-2001 (Per cent)	*The rate of production growth between 2001-2003 (Per cent)*	*Production volume in 2003 (in 10 thousands)*	*Profit and tax index for one unit (in 10 thousands)*
	14.5	69	113.71	3.56

Source: Author's calculations.

Note: The benefits from hard learning refer to those profits that have been obtained now, but could have been taken away by multinational enterprises, due to the substitution of multinational enterprises for domestic firms.

1 The share of foreign enterprises is about 46.82 per cent. See China Association of Auto Manufacturers (2003): *Economic Operation of the Auto Industry in 2002 and Development Analysis for 2003*, p. 8, January.

VI. CONCLUSIONS AND IMPLICATIONS

The following conclusions have been drawn from this case study of China's car industry:

First, Chinese domestic enterprises have vied with one another in order to enter into joint ventures or import new car models in the broad context of China's accession to the WTO. Even enterprises currently engaged in independent development and having their own brands are ready at all times to launch into joint ventures with multinational enterprises. To seek joint ventures, import new car models and to link up with multinational enterprises have become strategic options by domestic enterprises.

Second, with the progress of investment and trade liberalization concomitant with China's accession to the WTO, multinational enterprises have displayed their competition advantages to the full. Domestic enterprises have become increasingly attached to multinational enterprises as investment have expanded, technical levels have enhanced, and an increasing number of new products have quickly found their way into the market and prices of products have dropped.

Third, given the strategic adjustment of multinational enterprises and local firms and the changes in the relative competitive advantage between multinationals and local firms on the local market after WTO accession, China's car industry is being transformed into a dependent development model. In the absence of strong policy changes, what happened in the Latin American car industry could happen once again in China (Jenkins 1984, 1987; Evans 1995 and UNCTAD 2000).

Finally, the following lessons can be drawn from this case study:

First, given the almost unchallengeable competitive advantage enjoyed by multinationals, the development of infant industry and local firms of developing countries must be protected by government policy. Otherwise, infant industries and small firms cannot survive or develop healthily. In this sense, the extent, the scale and speed of trade and investment liberalization must match the capacity of local firms and industries and should be consistent with the learning, adapting and adjusting abilities of local firms and industries. Liberalization that is too rapid, profound, far-reaching would thus have a disastrous impact on local enterprises. Similarly, applying a "non-discriminatory" principle (National treatment and MFN Clause) to the area of investment where the level of competitiveness is so far apart, results in none other than contain the industries of developing countries.

Second, government or policy protection is only one of the necessary conditions to provide adequate conditions for local industry and firms to develop healthily. Under the market economy, firms will manage to earn money in the easiest and most profitable manner. This is also true for the protected market whereby an enterprise could benefit from market protection and not engage in product development and technological innovations, as well as any other capacity building activities. Therefore, the incentives and encouragements of government policies, internal competition among local firms, and the establishment of the interactive learning relationship between local firms and the multinationals are crucial for local firms and industries to be further developed in the context of closed markets (Evans 1995 and Porter 1990).

In view of this situation, we recommend that in the new round of multilateral trade negotiations, the Government should resolutely and unequivocally oppose the attempt by developed economies to incorporate investment issues into the multilateral trading framework and expand the "non-discriminatory" principle in the multilateral trading system to investments.[14] Auto industry cases show that enterprises of developing economies cannot challenge multinational enterprises without the necessary protection and support of their respective governments. We should not harbor any illusion about this. Our survey and research show that, if there were no requirements for technology transfer from multinational enterprises, joint ventures would be just a producing or assembling unit. It would be very hard for local product development ability to build up. Moreover, the Government should update the industrial policy of the automotive industry and encourage, or even oblige local firms to build their capacity and develop new product and technologies.

---

[14] Although China's WTO accession conditions associated to FDI might not be altered in line with the outcome of future multilateral trade negotiations.

REFERENCES

Cyhn JW (2002). *Technology Transfer and International Production – the Development of the Electronics Industry in Korea.* Cheltenham, Edward Elgar.

Evans P (1995). *Embedded Autonomy: States and Industrial Transformation.* Princeton, NJ, Princeton University Press.

Evans P, Frischtak C and Tigre P (1992). *High Technology and Third World Industrialization: Brazilian Computer Policy in Comparative Perspective.* University of California at Berkeley.

Fransman M (2000). Commentary. In: Kim Linsu Kim and Nelson RR. eds., *Technology, Learning and Innovation: Experiences of Newly Industrializing Economies,* 216–236. Cambridge, MA, Cambridge University Press.

Gerschenkron A (1962). *Economic Backwardness in Historical Perspective.* Cambridge, MA, Harvard University Press.

Hong Song and Chai Yu (1999). TNCs and industrial development in developing countries (in Chinese). *Reform,* 1999, No. 4.

Jenkins R (1984). *Multinational Corporations and Industrial Transformation in Latin America.* London, Macmillan Press.

Jenkins R (1987). *Multinational Corporations and the Latin American Automobile Industry.* London, Macmillan Press.

Kim Linsu and Nelson RR, eds. (2000). *Technology, Learning , and Innovation: Experiences of Newly Industrializing Economies.* Cambridge, MA, Cambridge University Press.

Krugman P (1994). The myth of Asia's miracle. *Foreign Affairs,* December, 62–78.

Krugman P (1997). Whatever Happened to the Asian Miracle? In: http: web.mit.edu/krugman/www/perspire.html.

Krugnman P (1998). What Happened to Asia? In: http:weh.mit.edu/ krugman/www/DISINTER.html.

Lu Ji'an (1999). *Take a Step Forward First – Selection of Localization Cases of Santana and Other Cars* (in Chinese). Shanghai Financial and Economics University Press, 1 July.

Nelson RR (1987). Innovation and economic development: theoretical retrospect and prospect. *Economic Journal,* 84(336):886–905.

Nelson RR and Pack H (1999). The Asian miracle and modern growth theory. *Economic Journal,* 109:416–436.

Poon Teresa Shuk-Ching (2002). *Competition and Cooperation in Taiwan's Information Technology Industry: Inter-Firm Networks and Industrial Upgrading.* Quorum Books.

Porter ME (1990). *The Competitive Advantage of Nations.* New York, The Free Press

UNCTAD (2000). *The Competitiveness Challenge: Transnational Corporations and Industrial Restructuring in Developing Countries.* United Nations, New York and Geneva.